KORNO SIGA,

THE MOUNTAIN CHIEF;

OR,

LIFE IN ASSAM.

MRS. MILDRED MARSTON
(MRS. Anna Kay Scott)

GYAN

Published by

GYAN

Gyan Publishing House
5, Ansari Road
Daryaganj, New Delhi-110002
Phone: 011-47034999, 9811692060
E-mail: books@gyanbooks.com

Distribution Network
gyanbooks.com
India, USA, Canada, UK, Australia, France

ISBN: 978-81-212-8738-8 (PB)
First Published, 1889

2nd Impression 2023

Printed at: Gyan Press, Delhi.

KORNO SIGA

Author: Mrs. Mildred Marston (Mrs. Anna kay Scott)

KORNO SIGA,

THE MOUNTAIN CHIEF;

OR,

LIFE IN ASSAM.

BY

MRS. MILDRED MARSTON.

WITH AN INTRODUCTION BY THE HON. JAMES M. HOYT.

PHILADELPHIA:
THE AMERICAN SUNDAY-SCHOOL UNION,
1122 CHESTNUT STREET.

NEW YORK: 8 AND 10 BIBLE HOUSE.

AFFECTIONATELY DEDICATED TO

MY CHILDREN;

WHO DURING ALL THE YEARS OF MY WIDOWHOOD HAVE BEEN BEAUTIFULLY LOYAL TO THEIR FATHER'S MEMORY,

AND TO

THEIR MOTHER.

CONTENTS.

PREFACE.

A PERSONAL acquaintance for many years with the author of this book, gives me full warrant to assure its readers that its recitals of missionary life and experience may be implicitly accepted as true.

The volume is not an imaginative portraiture of characters and events, said—in the ordinary phrase—to be "founded on fact," but it portrays from actual life the facts of missionary labor and experience as they occurred. The sole exception to strict verity is that the persons acting appear under assumed instead of their real names. For this substitution there were in the view of the author valid reasons: First; that as an active participant, yet living, in the labors, dangers, trials, sorrows, joys and spiritual achievements portrayed, the narrator would be thus shielded from what might, otherwise, be deemed undue self-assertion. Second, and more important; as a missionary of ripe experience the author could not otherwise present, with the warm commendation justly deserved, the noble and precious fruits and attainments seen in the lives of converts from heathen degradation to the purity and liberty wherewith Christ had made them free, without hazard of possible spiritual injury to some still living in the field referred to who might be unduly elated by such public praise.

For these reasons I take pleasure in presenting for my friend this explanatory preface; a pleasure, also, heightened by my estimate of the rare value of the narrative itself. As an earnest of its practical usefulness I add that my own heart, I trust, has been quickened by it to renewed and deeper interest in Christian missions to the heathen.

The recital in this narrative of God's call to a missionary life in heathen lands, and the thoughtful, prayerful, and at length loyal response to that call, and the precious spiritual results ensuing, signally verify the beautiful recognition of a divine overruling in the psalm of Whittier:

> "That more and more a Providence
> Of love is understood,
> Making the springs of time and sense
> Sweet with eternal good."

JAMES M. HOYT.

CLEVELAND, O., *Aug.* 12, 1889.

KORNO SIGA,

THE MOUNTAIN CHIEF.

CHAPTER I.

HOW IT CAME ABOUT THAT I WENT TO INDIA.

FOR several years my children have been urging me to write the story of my life in India. But as I am no writer, and have all my life been a hard-working woman in other fields save that of literature, I have hesitated much before undertaking this task. I have consoled myself, however, with the thought that the little book may be of interest to my children and personal friends, even though it is never so fortunate as to appear in print.

When I was quite a little girl, I thought a great deal about the people of that far-off land. My father was a great reader and a cosmopolitan, though he was a farmer and had never travelled beyond the confines of the United States of America. He used to talk with me about the books he read and tell me most interesting stories of the strange peoples in foreign countries. And I always was especially interested in the people of India.

My father was an earnest Christian man and deeply interested in the civilization and Christianization of the peoples of the earth, and I can never forget the stories he told me of Xavier, Marshman, Carey and Judson. And I would sit for hours wondering about all these things. As I grew older I read everything I could find about the people of India, and when I learned how ignorant and unhappy the women and children were, I wondered if it would ever be in my power to help them and in any way to better their condition.

At times I fancied myself embarking for "India's coral strand," and in imagination saw my relatives and friends bidding me a tearful farewell as I left them to sail away over the seas. Many a time did I go into my mother's bed-room and bolt the door, and softly sing to myself an old hymn which I found in my mother's Psalmist:

> "Yes, my native land, I love thee,
> All thy scenes I love them well;
> Friends, connections, happy country,
> Can I leave them far in heathen lands to dwell?
> Yes, I hasten from thee gladly;
> Lovely native land, farewell."

The years of my childhood passed rapidly and

happily away, and at the age of eleven I entered the academy of my native town, still hoping that the time might come when I could make my home in India. My eldest brother, who was my teacher in the academy, took much interest in my intellectual development, and it was a sad loss to me when he fell a victim to cholera on the 18th of July, 1851.

My next teacher was a much-beloved pastor, in whose judgment I had great confidence. During the winter following my brother's death a new minister, who was candidating for a church, talked to the children of our Sunday-school on Sunday at the close of the session. His words made a deep and lasting impression upon me, and I well remember these words as he urged the children one and all to "seek the Saviour early;" for the promise was, that all such should find him. After the Sunday-school closed I heard the deacons and other members of the church criticising my good minister, and calling him "poky." One of the deacons remarked, that such a stupid man would be obliged to travel a long distance before he would find a church that would settle him as their pastor. And all the while my young heart was pleading for him as the one minister that had spoken words more forcible and impressive than all others. I have never seen that so-called "poky" man from that day to this, but if I am ever permitted to look upon his face in a better world, where none are "poky," and where poor ministers do not have to go around candidating for churches which cruelly criticise them, I shall take his hand and tell him that he was the means of leading me out of nature's darkness into the sweet light of a faith in a risen Christ. Moreover, I shall tell him that the sheaves I have gathered in India and elsewhere, have all come from the seed he sowed long ago in that little country Sunday-school, where the deacons all thought he would never do any good.

When I was about seventeen years old, and just before I left the academy, my teacher urged upon me the importance of the study of the Greek language, and gave me to understand that he thought I would need it very much some day in translating languages in foreign countries. I was much surprised that he should have thought of such a future for me, for I had never told him of what my thoughts had been with reference to this subject. Indeed, I was very reluctant that any one should know I had thought of going to India, for I had become acquainted with a young man who interested me more than did the people of India. He was handsome, good and intelligent, and by the time I was nineteen years old had succeeded in convincing me that it was more important that I should look after his physical and spiritual well-being than that I should go on an Indian mission, and scatter my efforts among the Hindoos. He being present to urge his claims, got the better of the poor East Indians in the argument; for they, poor things, were far away in the jungles eating grasshoppers and chewing the betel-nut. And so I promised Theodore Osborne that I would be his wedded wife provided I could quit thinking it to be my duty to go to India. He said he would take me to our western frontier and give me a chance to work for the North American Indians, if I must work for Indians of some kind, and thus I could at the same time make him supremely happy. In order to satisfy conscience fully, which by the way has always been a very troublesome part of my organization, I made a solemn vow before my God that if I ever had a son I would name him either Carey or Judson, and train him from his earliest infancy to be a missionary to India. "And a man can do immeasurably more good than a woman, and hence this plan will be far better than if I went myself," I argued with my conscience. There were times when I would be intensely angry at this Indian question for continually presenting itself to me. I did not see why the other girls of my acquaintance should not be treated to an occasional dose of it. They never seemed to be burdened with such a thought, and could love and wed whom they chose.

During the summer of 1859 I bade my intended

husband a brief farewell, and went with a dearly loved sister to visit our uncle's family in the northern part of our State. There we had a most delightful visit with our young cousins and friends. We scoured the country for caves and natural curiosities generally, and spent pleasant days in fishing and hunting.

One Sunday morning a large and gay company of us went to a rude little church in the woods. We had been having a very hilarious time as we drove through the grand old forest, and I was in no reverent nor devotional frame of mind as I entered the church. Indeed, if I must tell the whole truth, I had shunned churches for months, fearing that I might hear something there that would cause my conscience again to clamor for the East Indians. How well I remember saying to myself as I ascended the church steps that morning: "Well, I shall not hear anything about foreign missions here: it is too far out in the woods for them to know or care anything about India."

The preacher was a young man of about thirty years, a professor of Latin in a neighboring college, of prepossessing personal appearance and withal a fine scholar. So absorbed was I, however, in my own reflections that I did not observe him until he announced his text: "Go ye into all the world, and preach the gospel to every creature," etc.

Every word of that sermon went to my heart, and after this long lapse of years I can recall sentence after sentence, which seemed intended for me personally. From that moment my old convictions returned with double power, and I was compelled to reconsider the subject and have it out with my conscience. I almost wished that I had been born without a conscience. I dared not tell any one of the fearful mental struggle through which I was passing, and though I frequently met the young preacher, I did not deem it wise to unburden my heart to him. I was glad when our visit came to an end and we turned our faces homeward. My sister often asked me why I was so sad and self-absorbed, but I gave her no clue to my thoughts. The young minister and a cousin of ours went with us to our home, and it certainly was not for want of agreeable society that I was silent. As soon as I reached home I resolved that I would honestly decide this subject. I wrote to my former pastor and teacher, describing my condition by quoting the first three verses of the sixty-ninth Psalm. I asked him to tell me what I ought to do; could it be right for me to break an engagement with Mr. Osborne, when by so doing my heart would be broken in twain? My pastor's letter in reply I have before me now. It was a great help and comfort to me. It begins thus:

"Amid the changing scenes of this fleeting life

it is a comfort to God's children to know that his loving kindness never fails them;" and then it goes on to say how safe it is always to follow a conscience enlightened by God's Spirit, and that those who are thus led shall lack for no good thing. How much more those words mean to me now than they did then! I have tested them and found them true. To make my story as short as possible, I will only add that I resolved in a few days after receiving this letter that I would tell Mr. Osborne all about the experience through which I had passed, and ask him as a Christian man what he thought I ought to do. Had I not been aided by an unseen Power I think I never could have borne up during that trying ordeal. It nearly broke my heart to see my beloved so sorely grieved as he was, when he found that I still felt that I had a personal work to do in a distant land which would involve a separation from him. But in the midst of his sorrow this noble man was strong enough to say: Mildred, you must follow the path of duty without reference to me, even though my disappointment should kill me. I have no sense of personal duty to the heathen; you have, and God and your own conscience must decide your course of conduct. But I would like to ask you one question: has that minister who preached the sermon in that country church from the text, "Go ye into all the world," etc., got anything to do with your present state of mind? Is he going as a foreign missionary? I assured him that the minister had long been engaged to my cousin, and that he had not the slightest idea of going as a missionary. Moreover that if he were not engaged, and if he were going to India, I should never go with him but should go out single and as a teacher, if I went at all. This assurance seemed to relieve his mind, and he said that he thought that much of my mental agitation about it being my duty, arose from a nervous condition, and that he had but little doubt I would give up India when I had fully rested from my journey and was once quietly settled down to life with him.

On the Sunday following this conversation I took my Bible and shut myself in my room that I might seek guidance from the All-Father, in this important matter. I had reached a point when I was almost desperate, and there was no earthly being who seemed able to help me in making a final decision. Very solemnly impressed was I that my whole future happiness and usefulness depended upon the course I now took.

> "There is a time we know not when,
> A point we know not where,
> That marks the destiny of man
> To glory or despair."

An old proverb says: "To everything there is a season."

Shakespeare words the same thought somewhat differently:

> "There is a tide in the affairs of men,
> Which, taken at the flood, leads on to fortune;
> Omitted, all the voyage of their life
> Is bound in shallows and in miseries."

And I felt most sensibly that such a time had come in my own life. For hours I remained in agony of grief and perplexity that I had never before experienced. I could not turn my heart away from him whose love was my highest earthly joy. I could not get strength of will to say: "Thy will, O God, be done." And so I wrestled and prayed for guiding wisdom until a superhuman strength and calmness seemed to come to me which enabled me to say: "I can do all things through Christ which strengtheneth me." Phil. 4 : 13.

I opened my Bible with an earnest desire that the first sentence upon which my eyes should rest might tell me plainly my duty. Judge of my surprise when a clause of the twentieth verse of the fourth chapter of Lamentations met my gaze: "Under his shadow we shall live among the heathen." The word "Under" begins with a capital and the sentence is complete in itself. I had never before noticed the sentence, and it seemed to me almost like a revelation from heaven. At any rate it was the means by which

I positively decided to prepare myself for work in India, provided the way should ever open for me to go there.

In less than a month from this time, I was in a distant city attending college and pursuing those very studies which my good pastor and teacher had years before urged upon me. I did not see Theodore Osborne again until after he was happily married to one who was in every way better suited to him than ever I could have been. Although we thought when we plighted our troth that no two people ever loved as we did, I am sure that the depths of my heart's affection had never been touched with the tender passion, and that he and I each learned afterwards to love another person far more than we had loved each other.

And I was happier from this time than I had been during those years when I carried a self-accusing conscience and a smothering of personal obligation to my Master and his needy children in India. Far better was it, to follow the leadings of the Spirit, and trust to an all-wise Father to right the error I had made in making a wrong promise and selling my birthright. It is the duty of individuals as well as of nations to be true to their highest destiny. But many of Mr. Osborne's friends and some of my own, censured me severely for the course I then took. Some called me an unbalanced enthusiast; others said I was a crank and a fanatic, and that "I would see the day when I would give my head to have the love of such a man as Theodore Osborne; he was a hundred times too good for me anyhow." My own dear relatives, however, were in full sympathy with me and bade me a hearty "God-speed" as I went away to college.

When I returned home after graduating in my course of study, the way had not opened for me to go to India, and I joined my sister in teaching a private school, and became deeply interested in the progress of our pupils, who were a delightful class of about forty young ladies. My pastor's wife, ever a true friend to me, wrote in my behalf to the headquarters of missionary operations for our church, and told them of my desire to go as a teacher to India; and the good old secretary, who has long since gone to a better world, wrote in reply: "I can only bid the young lady to await the openings of Providence."

"There are some gifts that Heaven denies
  More blest withheld than richly given;
There are some storms that darkly rise,
More blest than all the cloudless skies
  That make another's earthly heaven.
We know not till the middle day,
  What tokens best befit the dawn;
The clouds that weep our morn away
Fit oft, for heaven's serenest ray,
  When the full strength of life comes on."

CHAPTER II.

I AWAIT THE OPENINGS OF PROVIDENCE.

I CONTINUED teaching in my sister's school, but all the while I was awaiting the openings of Providence.

Once I thought the door open for me, and set about an outfit for a residence in India. A lady of much experience in educational work in India offered me a position as teacher in one of her schools there, and wished me to sail at once. My father, more wise and cautious than I, insisted upon a thorough investigation of the lady's mental condition. From her letters to me, he had gained an evidence of what he thought a vagarious state, and he even suspected incipient insanity. And so he bade me wait a year before sailing, assuring me that if at the end of that time my estimable patron proved to be *compos mentis* he would offer no further objections. Meanwhile he made a most diligent and searching investigation, and found that several of her ancestors had been insane, and that two members of her family besides herself were hovering on the border land. Before the end of the year she was unmistakably insane and thus a door closed, instead of an opening of Providence, confronted me, and those who had regarded me as a crank, now hoped I would be cured of my wild notions and settle down at home like a sensible girl. I was now twenty-two years old, and though I was in haste to be on my way, I knew that even if I was delayed several years I should still be young enough to hope for many years' work in India. I never seemed to doubt but that I had a work to do there, and I felt sure that the Lord of the vineyard would see that I got there in his own good time and way. I continued teaching and was happy in my work.

And now there came to me a strange letter from one whom I had never seen. I copy it here:

"MISS MILDRED PRESCOTT:

"*Dear Madam:*—The accompanying note of introduction from the pen of an old friend of yours may be deemed a sufficient apology for what might otherwise be quite intrusive. You may have noticed my name connected with an appointment to work as a missionary in foreign lands. I have for over a year had the pleasure of a somewhat intimate acquaintance with your former pastor's wife, being permitted to enjoy her hearty co-operation in most valuable labor and advice during a revival of religion last winter. During conversations with her she has several times incidently spoken of you, and your adaptation to such a work as I have chosen. You will permit me, therefore, without further introduction, to propose the object of this note, trusting that no offence will be taken, however the proposition may be considered or strange it may appear. My interrogatory proposition is this: Is your devotion to our common Master's cause, its interest and extension, and your love for the heathen deep and strong enough to prompt you to leave hallowed associations, to forsake the protection and company of long-tried and well-loved friends, and commit yourself to the protection and confide in the fidelity of a comparative stranger in a distant land of labor and trial, and doubtless of privation, and perhaps persecution?

"If thus you judge after mature reflection, and can consent to the general proposition, you will allow me to make it more specific and personal by referring you to the following gentlemen:

[Here follows a long list of D.D. and LL.D. worthies.]

"If after such investigation as you think necessary, you shall choose to return to me a favorable reply to the general proposition, and to so much of that relating to me personally as may be done without committing yourself, it will give me pleasure with your consent to visit you in a few weeks, when, by a personal interview, the question can assume a more tangible form. I am not unmindful that this is a most momentous proposal if considered affirmatively, and it has only been after much thought and earnest prayer, that I have dared to enter upon a transaction which involves such interests not only to the parties concerned, but also to the kingdom of Christ. Whether the finger of Providence has pointed me to you or not, must be confirmed by the direction he shall point you. I will simply add that the time is short. I am to sail for India next June, but missionaries should be 'minute men,' should they not? May I hope to hear from you as soon as deliberate thought shall render a deliberate decision?

"Yours truly,

"HENRY C. MARSTON."

Strange letter this, and it required days of reflection before I reached a "deliberate decision."

I was very strongly prejudiced against a marriage for the sake of convenience, and most of all it seemed to me that a marriage made for the sake of getting a chance to go as a missionary was the veriest sacrilege. One of my college classmates had become the fifth wife of an old missionary in China, and when he had proposed to her he had asked her if she "was willing to lay herself on the altar of missions." I was so disgusted with her for becoming the fifth sacrifice of that kind that I vowed I would preach against such immolation as long as I had power to speak. Personally, I must know and love the man I married for his own intrinsic worth. What a terrible thing it would be to marry a man because he was a missionary, and find after I got to India that I despised him! I wrote to the friend who gave Mr. Marston the note of introduction to me and asked her all manner of questions as to his mental and moral excellence, and her reply was certainly all that I could desire. I did not write to any of those D.D.'s and LL.D's. What did they know about the kind of a husband that would suit me? They might commend him to me, because they wanted him to sail soon for India.

The letter which I wrote to Mr. Marston is before me now written in a cramped school-girl hand which I discarded more than a score of years ago. It reads thus:

"REV. HENRY C. MARSTON:

"*Dear Sir*:—Yours of the 9th of March came duly to hand. I have perhaps delayed longer in the answering of it than I should, considering how soon you must sail for India. The proposition is one of such vital interest to the parties concerned that I am still wholly unprepared to return either an affirmative or negative reply. I have for years stood pledged to go as a missionary to India, should the way be opened for me in such a manner that I could see God's hand leading me in that direction. Whether he is now opening the way for me to go in company with you, it is as yet quite impossible for me to say; but in view of all this uncertainty, if you still wish to visit me and talk the matter over frankly, you can do so.

"Yours truly,

"MILDRED PRESCOTT."

Three weeks from the date of that letter Mr. M. came to visit me. We had interchanged several letters, and hence did not meet as entire strangers. It was Saturday afternoon at three o'clock when he was announced. I had pictured him in imagination as being tall and of commanding appearance, with a high intellectual-looking forehead and large black eyes. In all these respects he was as I had imagined, except that his eyes were dark blue instead of black.

His powers as a conversationalist were rare, and he soon succeeded in interesting me deeply in himself, as well as in his chosen work. Indeed his work was what I had always been interested in when I would allow my better nature to guide me. He told me of his sainted mother and aged father, and how these dear parents had at birth consecrated him to the work of foreign missions, but had told him nothing of it until he had declared to his father his purpose to go as a missionary to India. His mother had died while he was still a student in college. The father, now beginning to feel the infirmities of old age and his whole heart being wrapped up in this his only son, had taken back the gift he had made and strongly opposed his son's becoming a missionary to distant lands. But within a few months past he had cheerfully given his consent, and was almost as enthusiastic in his son's plans as if he were himself going to India. Quite needless is it that I should tell you of all the conversation of that long-to-be-remembered afternoon. You could not be as much interested in it as I was.

He preached in our church the next day, and we again spent an afternoon together. All of my relatives were delighted with him. Thus the days passed until the morning came on which I was to give him an answer. I had arisen early and had gone for a walk in the garden before breakfast. I had not expected Mr. Marston to put in his appearance before ten o'clock. I was stooping down over a too-spreading juniper shrub which was crowding out some delicate plants, when a voice clear and strong came to my ears, "Well, Mildred, what word have you for me this morning?" He had come before breakfast, he said, that he might learn his fate, and naïvely added that he might never want any breakfast. We were both standing with downcast faces looking at that juniper shrub, as though all our hopes were centred in it.

He waited silently for my answer which was: "Oh, if you are to starve until I say what you wish me to say, then I have here and now an unqualified and positive 'yes' for you." He smiled as only he could smile and said, "Thank you: you have made me very happy."

At this point my father called us in for morning prayers, and my pastor being present he read the Scripture about Isaac and Rebekah, and I was quite sure there was mischief in his eyes when he repeated the verse: "Wilt thou go with this young man? And she said, I will go." Six weeks from that morning we were married in the village church where I had worshipped with parents and dear brothers and sisters from my childhood's days. And then amid tears, sobs and fond parting words we left our friends and started toward our distant home in the Orient. When Henry had asked my parents for me they had answered, "We know that the hand of the Lord is in this thing and we dare not say, no. Take her and may Heaven's richest blessing rest upon you both, my precious children." And thus it was that I awaited the openings of Providence.

CHAPTER III.

OUR VOYAGE TO INDIA.

"Dear is our native land,
And sweet the light of home,
And starlike is the band
In friendship's beauteous dome.
But a brighter morning star
Invites our footsteps on
To eastern climes afar,
To the land of the rising sun.
On, On, On!
Hope's bright and morning star
Invites our footsteps on
To eastern climes afar,
To the land of the rising sun."

ON the 20th day of June we sailed in a merchant vessel for Calcutta. Four months were we sailing upon the ocean without once setting foot on *terra firma.* I was the only woman on board, and Mr. Marston and I were the only passengers. The account which I had to settle with old Neptune required almost all of my time for the first two weeks. I was so deathly sick at times that I could think of no better disposal of myself than to beg that they would lower me into the sea until they found a place where the waves no longer tossed, and where my poor stomach might find a much-needed repose. But I proved to be a pretty good sailor in spite of my first dreadful experience.

From Mr. Marston's journal I copy the story of our voyage.

"*June* 20. After these weeks of preparation and of sad farewells we are come at length to the side of the great sea which separates us from our chosen work. This morning at nine o'clock we are on board a ship bound for Calcutta. A steam tug tows us out ten miles or thereabouts; we pick our way amid ships and water craft of all kinds and fashions, from small row-boats to ocean steamers. The sun with kindly rays gilds with beauteous tint the last vision our eyes may ever behold in our native land, and Boston slowly sinks from our lingering gaze. Good-bye, dear native land; to thee I owe much, but to my Saviour more. While to him I owe my first affection and my best service, thou shalt ever fill one of the pleasantest palaces of my heart. Fair and beautiful Columbia, a long good-bye! The breeze begins to freshen, the ship feels the burden of the canvas and bows under the pressure of the wind, as the trees of the forest. Mildred begins to look white about the mouth and retires to her 'shelf' for the night.

"*June* 23. I have been having a sore battle with the angry sea-god, and so has Mildred, poor girl. This perpetual rolling and rocking is enough to set one's head crazy; mine seems as though it would burst, and Mildred cannot raise hers from the pillow.

"*June* 24. This morning a feeling of gloom pervades our little community. About midnight one of our crew, a fine-looking sailor, went overboard. The wind was piling the sea in large waves and it was intensely dark, that nothing could be done to save him. Poor fellow, he had the 'horrors;' had been made drunk by those who thus entrap sailors to go on a long, undesirable sea voyage. When he came to himself he gave way to despair. He talked of his family, whom he had not seen for eight years; he walked the deck in a frenzied state, and then with a maniacal scream he threw himself into the wild, dark waters, another victim to alcohol. He who despoiled this man of his reason knows little and cares less what anxious wife and children await in vain his homecoming. 'Woe unto him that giveth his neighbor drink, that putteth thy bottle to him, and makest him drunken also.' Hab. 2 : 15.

"*July* 4. Longitude 33° 49′—Latitude 32° 31′. I am now so far advanced in nautical ability that I can take the ship's reckonings as well as the captain. Indeed the captain says, if the ship by chance should be left in my hands, I could take her safely into port. But I am not as yet sufficiently nimble as a sailor to climb the rope ladder to the mast head, nor can I tell yarns equal to the sailors. We have no fire-crackers nor Roman candles with which to celebrate this, our natal day of America, but have hoisted our grand old flag of the stars and stripes out here on the broad ocean fifteen hundred miles from land, and nearly two thousand miles from home. We have just passed a British ship and a Bremen brig, and we are proud to proclaim to them that we hail from 'the land of the free, and the home of the brave.'

"*July* 28. To-day we have passed many of those little shell-fish, the nautilus, which the sailors call 'Portuguese men-of-war.' They are beautiful little fellows with membranous sails spotted with blue and pink, which they hoist to the winds while they propel themselves by means of numerous tentacles which surround the mouth and stretch down into the water. A school of porpoises is playing leap-frog near our ship, and seem to enjoy the sport hugely. You have often read of the stormy petrel, or, as the sailors term it, 'Mother Carey's chicken.' These little birds have been with us ever since we got well out at sea. They are about the size of our American robin, of brown color; they have long legs and a short tail and are web-footed. Though we are a thousand miles from land they are all about our ship, never alighting day nor night, except as they stand with extended wings on the water as they eat something thrown from our ship. In stormy weather they are full of wild delight, playing antics of all kinds with the waves.

"*Sept.* 3. Imagine yourself tossed and rocked incessantly day and night for weeks, and with no escape from it. We have just come out of a severe storm, and we have realized all the terrible grandeur and greater awfulness of a storm at sea. The wind coming to us from the west in ever increasing gusts lifted up the waves in huge piles, which curved upon themselves and lashed the sea into a snowy white foam. As we gaze out upon the angry elements, the waves seem to fall upon each other like infuriated beasts roaring at their very impotence to resist the fury of the winds, which, as in malicious sport, snatch the foaming crests from their owners, and, tossing them into millions of atoms, scatter them like drifting snow through the air. Now we mount up on the crest of a huge wave, while, beneath us on either side, yawns a frightful gulf into which we shall soon slide rapidly down. As we gaze upward from the chasm the seas seem consulting as to the way they may most effectually destroy us. One wave more savage than the rest shivers our little cabin window, and deluges our berths and clothing in a most uncomfortable manner. We are rounding the Cape of Good Hope, and we have decided to call it hereafter Cape Despair. In the midst of the storm, as Mildred was standing in the cabin-door looking out upon the terrific storm, she espied a Dutch brig only a short distance from us, the storm causing the atmosphere to be almost black with its gloom, and the brig also in a trough of the sea so that none of the ship's crew had seen it. Mildred called out loudly, 'a vessel.' And the captain had barely time to turn the ship's course sufficiently to escape a collision. We could almost touch the brig as she passed us. But the storm with all its black fury at length subsided. 'The Lord on high is mightier than the noise of many waters, *yea, than* the mighty waves of the sea.' And the storm rolls by, and he stills the angry seas. It is in such seas and under such circumstances that faith plumes her wings, and the heart is borne up above the tumult towards God and immortality.

"*Sept.* 29. One hundred and one days have passed since we stood upon land, and only once during this long period have we even sighted land, and that was in the early part of our voyage when adverse winds drove us within sight of the little town of Macayo, on the eastern coast of Brazil. We could see the little houses covered with red tiles, but we could not land, and our ship was at once tacked for the southeastern seas. This 29th of September is the anniversary of the one great sorrow of my youth. Twelve years ago I lost a mother of rare worth and affection. 'She was not,' for her Father called her home. Years have not changed nor dimmed the love of my heart for that priceless friend. Few are the days even now which do not yield to me some precious remembrance of her. Who can estimate the value of a loving Christian mother?

"Have our friends at home wondered how we pass our time on ship-board? We have finished a careful reading of the New Testament in English, and nearly one-half of it in Greek, besides a considerable study of the Old Testament in English. For pastime, we have read two volumes of 'Recreations of a Country Parson,' 'Ishmael in the Wilderness,' and one or two of our best American histories. We wish to be prepared to defend American policy among the English whom we shall meet in India.

"We have also read with much interest 'India, Ancient and Modern,' and 'Science a Witness for the Bible." We are now reading 'Man Primeval,' and are reviewing the Epistle to the Hebrews in Greek. In all these, Mildred shows quite as much of interest and ability as any theological student of the sterner sex. Who dares say that a woman has not the mental capacity of a man? Henceforth I am a strong advocate for women's colleges, with the same course of study as that of colleges for men. Yea, I go further; I claim co-education for them whenever they desire it.

"We have also accomplished something in the way of needle work, having finished an elegant rug of bunting for our drawing-room in India. The various arts of seafaring life have engrossed an hour or two of our time each day, and it is quite a satisfaction to me to feel that I could take our ship into harbor if necessary.

"*Oct.* 5. To-day there is a huge shark following our ship, which fact is to our sailors a sure prophecy of evil. How superstitious they are! For example, not one of them, from captain to cook, could be persuaded to taste of flesh upon which the moonshine has rested; for, say they, 'the moon poisons it.' And they actually stared at me in amazement when I proposed to test their superstitious idea by breakfasting upon 'moon-struck' chops. The meat was hurled overboard at once.

"*Oct.* 20. Our long voyage is at an end, and to-day we once more set foot upon *terra firma.* We are in Calcutta, the city of magnificent palaces and of native squalor. We at once commence making our purchases for our home in Northern India; but we are hindered on every hand by the Doorjah Poojah, a Hindoo festival which engrosses every native heart and head. Sacrifices innumerable of goats and buffaloes are daily being offered, and the noise of the 'tam-tams' is deafening.

"*Oct.* 31. We are on board a government steamer to which are attached two flat-boats loaded with Coolies for the Assam tea-gardens. There are about five hundred of these Coolies crowded together in filth and wretchedness. The cholera is raging fearfully among them, and victim after victim is pushed off into the Ganges as soon as life is extinct. Bloated, putrid corpses are floating on the water, or are lodged among the brakes and tall jungle grass which line the low banks. And now as the shades of night gather the jackals come forth from their lurking places of the day, and howl hideously over these dead bodies, as they rend them in pieces and devour them.

"The moral and physical condition of the natives is simply deplorable. And yet we are told that the Hindoos have a religion quite as good as the Christian, and that there is no need of teachers and missionaries coming from Christian countries to teach these poor wretches a better way.

"The English officers who are our fellow-passengers are fond of casting slurs upon America and the Yankees.

"Mildred becoming quite angry with one of them at the dinner-table to-day, asked him to remember, that insignificant and barbarous as he seemed to think America to be, she had whipped England once, and was quite able to do it again. Whereupon said Englishman subsided.

"*Nov.* 28. We stayed last night in a bungalow on the banks of the Brahmapootra. A tiger was prowling about all night, and made several attempts to enter the bungalow. I tried to get a shot at him, but failed. The poor natives are in mortal terror of these animals, and never tire of sounding the praises of the white man's Christian rifle. This morning we welcome a crowd of our hill men who come to conduct us on our way, and we mount our elephants, hired for the occasion, and make our way through the jungles to our future home.

"*Nov.* 30. At home; a beautiful green spot, the bungalow built of bamboo and the roof covered with jungle grass! How pleasant to be at rest after these months of journeying by sea and by land!

"And now welcome work for the Master, and good-bye to my journal of sketches by the way. I send this off at once to the loved and loving ones at home, who are anxiously awaiting tidings from

"HENRY AND MILDRED MARSTON."

CHAPTER IV.

ASSAM AND THE ASSAMESE.

HENCEFORTH our home was to be in the province of Assam in Northeastern India.

The word Assam is of Sanscrit origin, and was originally written Ahom. This word means unequalled, and the Assamese people think there is no land in the world equal to Ahom, and no people who can rival the Ahoms.

The province is a rich and fertile valley with mountain ranges on three sides. The great Brahmapootra river, with sixty smaller streams, waters the province and renders it productive. Assam is said to contain more rivers than any country of corresponding area in the world. The soil yields abundant crops of rice and tobacco. Tea is also extensively cultivated, there being in 1885 over nine hundred thousand acres under cultivation, with an average of about three hundred pounds to the acre. This tea is well and favorably known in both England and America. Iron, coal, rubber, sugar and silk are also found in Assam. The huge rubber trees are abundant on the hills, and thrive well also on the plains.

They as well as the banyans are a great boon to a country where the intense heat of the sun makes ample shade-trees so very valuable. Patches of sugar-cane are seen in all the villages, as well as large gardens of the mustard plant, and the everywhere present red-pepper.

Little was known of Assam previous to the seventeenth century, up to which time its form of government seems to have been largely patriarchal, and the aboriginal tribes were the predominating power.

The early Aryans who invaded Assam were a company of herdsmen who came there from Central Asia, and were a widely different people from their descendants, the present inhabitants of Assam. This branch of the Aryans which we call Indo-Aryan, or Hindoo, drove the aborigines into the distant mountains, and from this time petty Aryan kings ruled the valley of the great Brahmapootra.

In the beginning of the seventeenth century the Mogul emperors endeavored to annex Assam to their Indian domains, but were bravely repulsed by the Assamese, who successfully repelled the invasion. From this time until 1770 there were internal dissensions, and the country declined in power and prosperity, being rent by civil wars. In 1770 the British aided the Rajah of Assam in putting down a rebellion, and as a compensation for acting as umpire they received a portion of the province.

During a war with Burmah, in 1826, the British again came to the aid of the Assamese, and from that date until this, the whole of Assam has been nominally under British rule, though many of the hill-tribes have defied the lion's power.

The "unequalled" Assamese say that they descended from the Hindoo god, Indra, who presides over the atmosphere, and to whom the other gods are all subordinate. Indra, they say, placed the sun in the sky and charged the clouds with water. One of their prayers to Indra begins thus: "Shedder of rain, granter of all desires, set open this cloud." The Brahmapootra river derives its name from two Sanscrit words—Brahma, the creator of man, and "pootro," son: the son of the creator. The tradition says that ages ago there was a great and sore drought in the land, and in their distress the people cried to the creator Brahma, and he in compassion sent down his son in the form of a river and thus saved the perishing people. Hence the river is sacred, and he who bathes in its holy waters is made acceptable to the gods.

The Brahmapootra takes its rise north of the snow-covered Himalaya mountains. "Him" is the Sanscrit for snow and "aloi" is a palace, Himaloi, a snow palace. The view of this range in the distance, as the rising sun shines upon it, is one of the grandest sights eye ever gazed upon. It presents the appearance of a beautiful city with golden spires and domes. No wonder that the common people really think it is the abode of the gods and regard it with all the awe and reverence of the ancient Greek for his Olympus !

From this dwelling-place of the gods, the Himaloi range, did the Creator send his son the Brahmapootra. To be thrown into this sacred river is to the Hindoo mind a sure guarantee of a better state in the next transmigration of soul. An old Assamese once told me that he would not for all the gold of India be buried under ground, as he would in this case surely become either a worm, snake or toad : whereas if he were thrown into the Brahmapootra, he stood a fair chance of being a fish, or a crocodile, either of which was much higher in the transmigratory scale. I have counted during the cholera season in one day a hundred corpses which had been thrown into the river. Some of them had been partially cremated according to the custom of the high cast Hindoos, but the greater part had been pitched into the river as soon as life was extinct.

Never shall I forget the impression made upon me by those bloated dead bodies as they floated in the river. And when night came and the boat anchored for the darkness, there was something intensely torturing in the hideous yells of the jackals as they fought over the bodies which had washed ashore.

Sleep visits not the "newly arrived" in India under such circumstances, and nerves and sympathies are racked until the morning light drives away the carnivorous herd. And yet long residence in India makes even the European somewhat indifferent to the ghastly sights. An old tea-planter laughingly asked me if I understood the words the jackals used, when making a feast from the dead body. "Listen," he said, "the first sentence is an announcement to the whole jackal tribe: 'Dead Hindoo—Dead Hindoo;' and the invited guests answer back 'where, where?' The original finder replies 'here, oh, here.'" Thus instructed I listened and was surprised to find how exactly their cries seemed to take on the form of the planter's words. The natives regard all this with supreme indifference, and when they saw my great perturbation, they would toss the head as only a Hindoo can, and say, "The gods have written the fate of all on their foreheads: if they have written there that one is to be eaten of jackals, that one is only fulfilling the destiny the gods have arranged for him. Who are we that we should fight against the gods?"

I am glad to say that the English government put a stop to this custom of throwing the dead into the rivers before I left Assam, and the natives either burn or bury their dead. Thus the river water which every one drinks (there are no wells in Assam) has become purer. The rivers of Assam abound in crocodiles, among which are many man-eaters. These animals are fond of basking in the sunshine on the banks of the river near the water's edge. Mr. Marston has frequently shot them from our little boat, and finding that the ball has lodged in a vulnerable spot, we have moored the boat and minutely examined these monsters, which often measure twenty feet in length. The natives are fond of crocodiles' eggs, which they unearth from the warm sand where the animal has deposited them, trusting to the sun's rays to hatch them. The crocodile's egg is about the size of a goose egg, and is said to be quite as palatable.

Many natives in Assam are yearly killed by the crocodiles. Yet in spite of all the risk, hundreds of men, women and children daily bathe in the rivers. I have often heard, in the stillness of the night, the loud champing of the monster's jaws, and felt the thud of his heavy body as he has struck our little boat, and springing to the children's bed to see if they were safe, the old native nurse starting up from her sleep would cry out, "Ki hol, mem saheb?" "What is the matter, white lady?" And when I would tell her there were crocodiles all about the little canoe, she would yawningly reply: "Well they can't eat your children unless the gods have foreordained them to become food for the crocodiles, and if these children were created for that purpose you ought not to fight against the gods. What is written on one's forehead must come to pass." And with these comforting words she would seek her mat and sink into peaceful slumber. Such is Hindoo fatalism. According to their creed everybody's fate is written on the forehead in letters so minute, that none but the gods can read them. Every event of life is chronicled there, and the infant at birth has its whole future thus laid out definitely by the gods.

The classical language of the Assamese is the Sanscrit, the most ancient and original of all the Indo-European languages and the one which throws much light upon the original roots of language.

This wonderful language opens to us the inward and the outward life of a people who number one-seventh of the human race, for it is the sacred language of all the Hindoos. The alphabet has ten distinct characters for the vowels, four for the semi-vowels, five nasals, ten surd mutes, ten sonant mutes, three sibilants and three aspirants, making in all forty-five distinct characters. This language is richer in declensions than the Greek, but poorer in conjugations. Our decimal notation and algebraical calculus are both derived from the ancient Hindoos. The Sanscrit is, however, a dead language, and the spoken language of the people of the plains is a derivation of the Ancient Sanscrit which varies as widely from the original as the modern Greek of to-day from the Ancient tongue.

The spoken language is called Präkrit, and is written like the Sanscrit from left to right, in characters which are made up of triangles and straight lines with very few curves. It is guttural like the German, and somewhat difficult for Europeans to speak. It was only after I had been in Assam two years, that I could make the natives understand whether I was talking to them about a house—ghor, a wall—gor, or a rhinoceros—gŏr (with the nasal sound). The Assamese is the language of the entire population of the Brahmapootra valley, and is the medium of intercourse with the bordering hill tribes, hence it must be learned well if a person wishes really to know the people who speak it, and hopes to benefit them. The Bengali language in common with the Assamese, borrows its religious and scientific terms from the Sanscrit, and on this account the two languages have been thought identical. But the grammars of these two dialects are quite different, and therefore they cannot be said to be one and the same language. We might as well consider the French and Italian languages identical, as they both spring from the Latin.

No people on the face of the earth suffer more

from evil spirits than the Assamese. I, of course, do not refer to those evil spirits by which thousands in Christian lands annually fill a drunkard's grave. Fortunately for the Assamese, the Hindoo religion forbids its followers from becoming possessed with this kind of spirits. The old Hindoo law commands that if a man be found guilty of drinking intoxicating liquor, he shall be compelled to drink the same quantity boiling hot. He does not often repeat the offence. And every respectable Hindoo community at the present day deems each drunkard worthy of being carried in derision through the streets with all the opprobrium of tar and feathers. Our land might well learn a salutary lesson from the Hindoos in this respect.

Demonology among the Hindoos dates back to the age of the Vedas. These books are believed to have been written as early as the time of Moses, and were collected in the fourteenth century B. C. Mount Meru, which stands between the earth and the heavens, is the battle-ground of the demons. Some of them are pictured with long tusks and bloody tongues, who lurk in secret places for human prey. Ogres, snakes with human faces, dwarfs, dragons and vampires are believed to be in every available space in air, earth and water. There is not a space in nature as wide as a hair which some evil spirit does not fill. The good spirits live far above the earth, and are not supposed to concern themselves much with human affairs. The demon "Oop" is one greatly feared by the ignorant. He is said to be a huge monster with a blood-red tongue a yard and a half long, and with tusks like an elephant, who has a disagreeable practice of stalking abroad every Tuesday and Saturday night in search of human victims. I have been most solemnly told by a frightened man that he had just escaped from "Oop;" that he had seen his tusks and his well-known tongue, and had felt his hot breath on his shoulders.

The "Evil Eye" is another demon who is supposed to be always peering about, and many are the artifices to which the people resort in order to evade him. An Assamese must not be looked at when he eats, lest the "Evil Eye" may be lurking through human eyes, and curse the food and the eater. The dining-room of the Assamese is necessarily the darkest room in the house, the one most retired from human gaze. You must never tell the Assamese woman that her child is beautiful, for the demons will hear you and carry off the child. On the contrary you may evade the demons and please the mother, by calling the child very plain, and at the same time giving the mother a wink, to let her know that you mean just the contrary to what you say. I have heard an Assamese mother call her new-born babe all manner of vile epithets, that the demons may be made to believe that the child is not worth their carrying away. They give their children repellent names for the same reason. One man who had lost several children called the last born "Ghin," which means "Hate," and this one lived. It was hard for him even after he became a Christian, to give up his belief that the odious name had saved to him this child. If a person rudely strikes a tree in which an evil spirit resides, or spits under it, the evil one will be sure to punish him sooner or later. Bamboo trees must be cut only on certain days of the week, for fear of offending the spirits.

The Assamese greatly fear the darkness, and will not leave a child asleep alone in a dark room, believing a demon will carry it off. As I was in the habit of putting my babe to sleep early and leaving it in a dark room, I have frequently heard the native women exclaim: "Hai, hai, mem lukh bhutor kotha na jane!" "Alas, alas, the white ladies know not the customs of the evil spirits."

It is distressing to witness the effect of this belief in demonology upon the children of the country. From their earliest childhood they listen to frightful stories of the depredations of evil spirits, and their young lives are robbed of half their comfort by the fears which continually assail them. A native quakes with fear, if by chance a vulture alights upon his house; it is a sure omen that one of his family will soon become the food of vultures. They say a young vulture can never fly until he has tasted of human flesh. A certain magistrate in Assam fined one of his subordinates quite heavily, whereupon the subordinate took the head of a male sheep, drove seven nails in it, and with many incantations buried it, at the same time expressing his firm belief that in seven days the magistrate's head would be in the ground.

The cholera is considered the worst and the largest of the demons, which walks by day and by night through the land, killing whomsoever he will. The name of this disease must be spoken only in a whisper during its prevalence in a village, and many speak of it as the "Great One."

An earthquake is caused by the shaking of the elephant upon whose back the earth stands.

These and many other superstitions which I have not time to enumerate are disappearing before the onward march of Christian civilization.

CHAPTER V.

THE HILL TRIBES OF ASSAM.

THE mountaineers of Assam are a widely different people from the Hindoos, whom the preceding chapter describes.

These hill tribes were doubtless once the inhabitants of the beautiful Brahmapootra valley, and were driven thence by the invading Aryans, the forefathers of the Hindoos.

The barren mountains and the wild jungles were deemed good enough for these aboriginal inhabitants of Assam. What if these people did prefer the fertile plains and green valleys? A stronger and more cunning race decided that these aborigines must go, and allow the conquerors to demonstrate the beauty of the "survival of the fittest." Very much after the same pattern have we Americans treated our aborigines. And we are yet far from perfect in following the divine precepts of the Christ, who taught us both by precept and example the true brotherhood of man.

Many and fierce were the conflicts, however, before the hill tribes relinquished their rights to their enemies. If physical strength could have decided the warfare they could have been victors, but when treachery and intrigue were brought to bear upon them they were outwitted by the crafty Hindoo.

Very few of these tribes had been reached by Christian influence or western ideas of civilization, when Mr. Marston and I went to live among them. They had no written language, no ancestral lineage of honor, and no very definite form of religious worship. They have a tradition that points to a Chinese origin, and the old people tell of a time when they had a literature and a name among nations.

But as they neglected the tilling of the soil, and gave all their time to their books, the mountain deities became angry, and gathered together all their books and made a huge bonfire of them, and from that time they have grown ignorant and barbarous.

The people among whom our lot was cast were more peaceable than the others, and never fought with their neighbors if they could escape it. Their dialect is almost entirely monosyllabic, and they use the same word for many different purposes: for instance, *hem*, is a house; *hem kong-long*, is a house on wheels, *i. e.*, a wagon. Their houses are made of bamboo and grass, and are built from twenty to thirty feet above the ground, the ascent being by rude ladders which are nothing more than unhewn trees, with notches cut in them for steps. An ordinary house costs them about two dollars, and requires about ten hours for its construction. The floor is of split bamboo, and bends under your foot at every step. The style of architecture is neither Gothic nor Ionic, but exceedingly aboriginal. The houses are long and narrow, and are destitute of all kinds of furniture. The roof is thickly thatched, and projects several feet beyond the sides of the house.

The soil is not fertile like that of the plains, and the quantity of rice raised is not sufficient to feed the inhabitants. Cotton is, however, an abundant product of their soil, and this they exchange for rice when they visit the plains.

The women weave a coarse cotton cloth, coloring it either blue, red or yellow, and of this material the garments of both sexes are made. The dress of the women is a short blue petticoat extending from the waist to the knees, while the male attire is even more limited, being a short apron of red cotton cloth. For the cooler weather, they add a red cotton shawl fringed at both ends, and worn as the Hindoos wear the *chuddar*, *i. e.*, one end over the head, and the other falling gracefully over the shoulders.

Both sexes are very fond of mustard oil as a pomatum, and you can make a mountain chief no more acceptable present than a bottle of mustard oil. This use of it has, however, been learned of the Hindoos. In their native state, these mountain people are the most unkempt of all the Asiatic races. They also use the mustard oil in cooking their meats and vegetables. Yams and sweet potatoes are cultivated with considerable success, and are roasted in the ashes as our grandmothers used to cook Irish potatoes. Fish is in great demand. The mountain streams yielding but very few, the people are often under the necessity of substituting grasshoppers' and elephants' flesh for them.

Wild, ignorant and filthy as these children of the jungle are, there are characteristic traits pertaining to them which strongly attach them to those who are interested in their civilization and Christianization. Their trust and simple faith in their teachers and superiors are at once a comfort and an inspiration. They are not idolaters, have never had any images of their gods, and are much less superstitious than the Hindoos. They worship the sun, the god of disease, the spirits of their ancestors, and the Great Spirit. Their mode of worship is almost entirely by sacrifices of vegetables, rice, chickens and goats. Often have I seen a toddling infant among them carry his little handful of rice, and offer it at the root of some large green tree, believing as he had been told, that some god lives in that tree and will bless the giver of even a handful of rice.

As we have before remarked, there is little doubt that these mountain tribes once inhabited the plains, and lived in a greater degree of civilization and refinement. But the ancient Aryans invading the country in the remote ages drove these unsuspecting people, by treachery, back into the barren mountains and cheated them of their long possessed country. In the same selfish manner did our most revered Puritan fathers treat the North American Indians. And we, as their descendants, have as yet learned but little more of that true spirit of Christian philanthropy that would lead us to love our neighbor as ourselves.

In all that pertains to the comforts and elegancies of civilized life, these tribes inhabiting the mountains of northeastern India are poor indeed.

Vermin of all kinds live luxuriously among them, and often after entertaining a company of these people in my drawing-room, I have seen twenty and more of the species *Cimex* creeping away from where my guests have been seated. Six or seven of these loathsome bugs are given internally by the people to prevent ague.

Fleas also abound, and during the months of March and April, they seem literally to take possession of our houses. On arising from our beds an armed host seemed to attack our feet, covering them so thickly that we could hardly discern by sight, whether they were human flesh or parasitic fleas. The dust of the earth during these two months swarms with them, but as the rainy season sets in they disappear as if by magic.

The mountain jungles abound with mammoth trees: oaks, chestnuts, and birches thrive on the higher ranges, and lower down we find the rubber, the teak and the *hal.** Here and there all over the hills are acacia trees, and the use of the bark is well recognized by the natives.

Wild animals abound in the dense jungles, and human life is not safe while travelling even short distances. The huge man-eating Bengal tiger has found his way into these mountains, and is ever on the alert for human flesh. The elephant, rhinoceros, the buffalo and the bear are numerous, and leopards, jackals and monkeys are as thick as peas in a pod. Birds of gorgeous plumage abound, but we miss the sweet singers of our native land; the only singers I have met among the birds of India being the *mina* and the *bim raja.*

* The *hal* or *sal* (for the natives use "h" and "s" interchangeably) is a hard wood. We used to call it the Assamese mahogany.

CHAPTER VI.

OUR MOUNTAIN HOME.

SHOULD I live to be a hundred years old I can never forget the day when we reached our home on the mountains.

Fifty swarthy, robust hill men came to meet us, and to conduct us on our way. When the mountain paths became too steep for our elephants, these men carried us in baskets, on their shoulders, with a strap passing across their foreheads. The hill men are wonderfully strong, and can climb the mountains with the agility of the wild goat.

Thus at length we came, after perils by sea and by land, to our chosen home among the hill people of Assam. We were the first white people that had ever attempted to make a home among them, and I was the first white woman they had ever seen.

Our hearts were deeply touched by the warmth and kindness of our reception. They had cut bamboo and thatch and with their own hands built us a dwelling-house and also a chapel and school-house. And though in our eyes they were rude, empty structures, they were palaces to these ignorant people.

We at once set about learning the language by making use of every word we heard, and putting it into a vocabulary for future use. A missionary who had travelled through this section had made a list of words, and this we found very useful. And having no interpreter we were quite astonished to find ourselves in a few months successful in conveying instruction to the ignorant ones about us. They were entirely ignorant of the most common laws of health and cleanliness, and we had need of much patient endurance in well-doing.

At the end of the second year among them, we had gathered a flourishing Normal School in which were taught young men of seven different tribes. These were all preparing to go out as teachers and Bible readers among their respective tribes. I had found it almost impossible at first to get the parents' consent for their daughters to be instructed. They would laugh heartily at the absurdity of the idea and exclaim, "Teach the girls! Why you might just as well gather in the goats and the wild hogs and seat them on benches, and teach them the alphabet." But by means of attractive music, bright-colored jackets, and a bottle of mustard oil, I at last won my way into their hearts and thus started my first girls' school. What pleasure I found in opening to them the doors of knowledge, and how good and true they were to me!

A savage, warlike tribe inhabited the hills north of our peaceable tribe, and as we daily looked out upon these blue ranges we longed to carry to them also the message of peace and eternal life. English officers one after another had been murdered by them, and hence every one warned us as we valued our lives to keep away from these savage people. In spite of all these warnings my good husband resolved to make the venture. The English magistrate offered him an escort of sepoys and the protection of the English army, but he politely declined this assistance, saying quietly, "For me 'it is better to trust in the Lord than to put confidence in princes.'" The voice of his Master seemed plainly to say to him, "Go teach them also," and he dared not disobey the heavenly vision; indeed he was eager to obey it. An event which was of momentous interest to us occurred about this time, and hence Henry delayed his hazardous journey to those northern savages. I will copy from Henry's letter to his home circle describing this important event. "The Lord has been pleased to send to us a missionary associate in the person of a baby-boy. There being no physician within several days' journey of us, you may imagine that we felt much anxiety about the issue of the event, especially as we have no trusty old women nor nurses. So I took my Bible and read, 'What time I am afraid I will trust in thee,' and then I took my 'Household Practice of Medicine' and tried to follow out the directions given there, and the results were all we could have wished or asked for. As for the boy himself, he is a fine young fellow and asserts his claims most vigorously. They say he looks like his father, but I think he is more like Mildred. We call him Paul.

"That God should make over to us in trust such great interests as cluster about an immortal spirit reminds us most forcibly of what he expects us to be and to do. How honored every parent is! and yet I shrink from the responsibility. But now there is no option. Already by our command, under God, a frail bark has been launched on the great sea of an endless life; the immortal spirit waiting by the shore, the moorings cut, sails unfurled, anchor weighed, waiting for our hand to take the helm and pilot it through the straits of infancy and youth, over the quicksands, and by the rocks out into the open sea with a well-planned chart for further guidance and direction. Oh, for wisdom and patience to do all this aright!"

And now I will go back to my history of Henry's trip to the tribes north of us. Our little Paul was three months old, and as the natives all about me were very kind and attentive, Henry felt that baby and I would be cared for during his absence. How sad I felt that morning when he said, good-bye! I feared that I should never see him again. I dared not go with him on account of our baby. And so with tearful eyes I gazed after him and his faithful band of school-boys. What might not those savage people do to him? How would they receive him and his strange message of a crucified Christ?

After two weeks' journey he came to a narrow pass between two rugged mountains. And as he attempted to enter that defile and thus set foot upon the soil of the savages, he was confronted by a band of twenty warlike chiefs painted with hideous colors, each wearing a necklace of human skulls. These chiefs instantly ranked themselves into two squads of ten each, and standing in a line at the entrance of the defile they lifted their long spears above their heads and defied the missionary and his little unarmed band. For one moment only did Henry hesitate; then taking his violin, which he had called during all our residence in Northern India his second assistant in missionary work, he drew the bow and in a calm and clear voice accompanied the instrument in a language understood by the chiefs, and sang, "Am I a soldier of the Cross," etc. The savages listened with rapt attention until he had marched slowly through the defile and past them and their uplifted spears, and as he sang and played, one after another of the spears were dropped and their owners seemed completely under the magical spell of the music and the man. As the music ceased an old chief, who was their leader, exclaimed: "It is a god and not an Englishman, and see, the instrument he carries is alive and has a voice like the *bim rajah.*" The *bim rajah* is their sweetest bird songster.

"Stranger, wherefore come you amongst us?" is the question they finally ask.

The missionary realizes that his life probably depends upon his answer to that question, and he carefully chooses his words.

"I come to teach you to sing and play on this violin with which you are so much delighted. I come to help you to be wise men and to live as other great nations live; to give you a written language and books, and a better religion than what you now have."

"Are you an Englishman?" they ask.

"No, I am an American, and have nothing to to do with the setting up of a new government among you."

"What is that strange creature you carry about that sings so sweetly?"

"It is a musical instrument which in Christian countries is called a fiddle or violin."

"Well, stranger, you may come and live here

among us if you will bring that 'Christian fiddle' and teach our sons how to use it."

And thus it was that the missionary, by means of a violin, gained an entrance among a people who before this had cruelly slain every white man who had ventured among them. He stayed two months among them, and taught them the words of eternal life, and the story of the Son of God. When he returned home six of the young men of that tribe came with him to study in our Normal School, and to go back as teachers and Bible readers among their people. And thus it was that a wide door was opened for us among that hitherto barbarous tribe; a work which has been developing and widening during all the succeeding years.

My husband went from place to place among the people of the villages and in the jungles much of the time, while I remained at home to look after the schools and our little family. When Paul was three years old a winsome little daughter whom we called Ruth came to us. We were very happy in our home life—happier, I think, than four-fifths of the families in America and England—though we lived in a bamboo house, with mudded walls, and had no carpets and no "interior decorations." For, we felt that we were doing a work which was benefiting humanity, and which would never have been done but for us.

Our lives were counting for something, and we were polishing rough stones for the temple of the living God.

It is true we were exposed to hardships, and the plague was often rife in our midst. We ministered day and night to the sick and the suffering during the cholera epidemics, and felt no fear. Is not man immortal until his work is done? And did not Christ our example thus spend his life as he went about doing good? And should the servant be more chary of his service than his Master? We came very near losing our precious Paul with that dreadful disease of India, jungle fever. None but parents can know our anxiety as we watched beside him day after day, fearing that the sweet young life was going out. How we longed for a good physician, who would advise us as to his medical treatment! Brain fever set in after the jungle fever had lasted three weeks, and the poor little fellow's screams were most pitiable. Never shall I forget the night when the crisis came. He fell into a quiet slumber, and when he awoke his fever was gone, and he recognized us. Henry and I both fell upon our knees, and breathed out our hearts in grateful thanksgiving. Our young men of the Normal School, after three years' instruction, had gone out to teach among their people, and as Mr. Marston travelled from place to place he found many who were ready to be taught, and these one after another entered the school, so that we always had as many pupils as we had funds to provide for.

Many were the perplexities I had in getting a girls' school on a firm footing. The parents did not realize the importance of educating the girls in book knowledge, and I was hence obliged to teach needlework, spinning, weaving, and the cutting and making of garments. Often a crusty old father could be induced to send his daughter to me for instruction, by looking at a handsomely embroidered pair of slippers, and learning that if he would only let his daughter Kache come to school, she could make him a pair just like those. Many a faithful native worker in India to-day owes his or her Christianization to a slipper! "Upon Edom will I cast my shoe. . . . . Who will bring me into the fenced city? who hath led me unto Edom?" (Ps. 108 : 9, 10, Revised Version.)

Early one morning there came to our bungalow a man of imposing figure and noble bearing. He led by the hand a little child, a boy about six years of age. On seeing us he advanced, and with a low salaam addressed us thus: "I am a chief. I live far away in the jungle. I have heard that you have come from the setting sun to teach us hill men about the great God. I am now old, but my children can learn the true religion. Here is my youngest son. I give him to you. Take him. He is no longer mine, but yours. Where you go, he shall go; where you stay, he shall stay; your religion shall be his religion, your God be his God. But he is a little child. Be kind to him for his parents' sake, for we love him dearly."

Thus saying he quietly turned to his child for a last fond embrace, and in a moment, without waiting for a reply, was out of sight on his way back to his distant jungle home. I mention this incident to show how the people were coming to have confidence in us, and in the work we were doing for them. This boy proved to be one of our brightest pupils in the Normal School, and a great comfort up us.

CHAPTER VII.

KORNO SIGA, THE MOUNTAIN CHIEF.

MR. RUSKIN in his preface to "The Story of Ida" says: "The lives we need to have written for us are of the people whom the world has never thought of, far less heard of, who are yet doing most of its work, and of whom we may learn how it can best be done." The hero of our story, though an unknown man of the jungle, comes under this class, and this is my only apology for attempting to write some of the incidents of his life.

Korno Siga was born in a small rude village on the mountains. His name is derived from the Assamese language and means, "split-ear." His father was a mountain chief, but very poor in this world's goods.

When his mother bored the ears of her baby-boy according to the custom of all respectable aborigines, the instrument slipped and cut through the entire lobe of his right ear. As she knew nothing of surgery the ear was left to heal in its divided condition and he was named according to the deformity, a custom which prevails largely in

India. If a baby cries a great deal, he is apt to be called *Kandoora,* a cry-baby. If one smiles often, he is called *Milikia,* a smiler. The ear ornaments worn by these people of both sexes are enormously large and are often of the rudest character. They are made of wood, colored glass, or wads of cotton-wool, into which some large flower has been inserted. They are often so heavy as to pull the lobe of the ear until it touches the shoulder.

But little is known of Korno Siga's early years. When about eighteen years of age (these people keep no record of their children's ages and hence we never knew positively their age), he came to our mission station and learned to read and write. When he had been with us four months he became a convert to Christianity. The manner of his coming to us was as follows: one sultry afternoon during the prevalence of the Southwest monsoon, my husband and I were seated on the verandah, surrounded by a group of natives whom we were instructing.

Suddenly there appeared from the jungle near our house a wild, unkempt boy who rapidly urged his way through the crowd of mountain men on the verandah, and came to us. His first words were, "Are you the white teachers?" Being answered in the affirmative he made a low salaam and seated himself on the floor. In reply to our questions as to who he was, and what he wanted, he told the following story, which I give as nearly as possible in his own words:

"My name is Korno Siga. I come from the distant hills. I wish to know what the religion of the white man is and what it can do for a rude mountaineer. Mine has been a sad, hard life. When I was an infant I was swapped for a kid, because I was a frail child and my poor father and mother feared that I never could be of much service to them, either in cultivating the cotton, or working in the rice-fields. So they gave me to the family of another chief that was childless, and who preferred me to the kid. My foster-parents taught me to worship the mountain spirits, and to take my little handful of rice each morning and lay it at the root of some large green tree. They told me that the spirit who lived in the tree would thus be pleased with me, and keep the evil spirit of disease from me. I was taught to pay the highest respect and veneration to these trees. They were mostly the huge rubber trees with which our mountains abound. I was taught that it was very wicked to mar the trunk or branches of these sacred trees, and that if I spit underneath one of them, it was a direct insult to the gods who lived in their branches.

"Many hours did I spend under these trees trying to catch a glimpse of a god, and to learn if he was pleased with my offerings. But as I grew older I became more and more dissatisfied with myself and my mode of worship, and with the rude life of the mountaineers. I felt that there must be a manner of life higher and better than this, and I longed to visit the plains and talk with the Hindoo priests and religious mendicants and fakirs of whom I had heard. Perhaps they could tell me of a better way of living and of worshipping. About this time my foster-mother died, and her corpse was placed on the *chang* (a bamboo frame on which the dead are kept for a number of days before cremation or burial) for thirty days. The first fifteen days of this time her disembodied spirit was supposed to be roaming over the earth seeking a place of rest, and during this time hired mourners wept and wailed for her. The last fifteen days were spent in feasting and dancing, because the weary spirit was supposed to have found an abode in some other form of existence. Many a night did I go and sit in the darkness near my mother's *chang* until the day dawned. How I wished that she would speak to me and tell me what she had learned since she had left me! But no voice came to me through the stillness of the night, and I was unhappy and desolate in spirit. And hence I sought a Hindoo high priest, who lived at the foot of our mountain, and who claimed that he could make unhappy people happy. The journey was long and perilous, for the way was through a pathless jungle infested with wild and savage animals.

"The 'Great One of the Earth,' as he styled himself, did not receive me graciously, nor did his aspect impress me with a confidence in his purity and holiness of character. I told him the whole story of my life, and of my desire to obtain something higher and better than I had yet found. I asked him if he could tell me of some good thing I could do, whereby I might be able to forget all the wrong things I had ever done. He answered that all power and all knowledge were his; that being sinless himself he could forgive the sins of others; but that I must first commit to memory one thousand Hindoo *Slokas* (wise sayings of the Shasters), which he would daily rehearse for me; and immediately afterwards make two long pilgrimages to holy shrines. When all this had been done I must become his cow-boy, and be obedient unto him all the days of my life. I cheerfully promised to do all he had asked of me, if he would in return give me peace of mind and make me truly happy.

"Our people have wonderful memories, and it was not many weeks before I had the thousand *Slokas* so that I could repeat them in consecutive order, as given in the Shasters. But the pilgrimages were hard indeed. The first required that I should have nails driven through the soles of my wooden sandals, and at every step the blood flowed from my pierced feet, and I could only take a few steps at a time, and then wait days for the wounds to heal before I resumed my journey. Thus I was months making my first pilgrimage and at length reached the spot sacred to all Hindoos, where I threw myself prostrate before the idol, and begged that he would give me an assurance that all I had done was acceptable to him. I tore my hair and smote upon my breast and cried yet more loudly, but no voice spoke to me and no smile of compassion lighted up the grim visage of the god. Weary and discouraged, I made my way back to the priest, and asked him what more I should do. He ordered my second pilgrimage to be made by measuring my length to another shrine. I would that I could have escaped another weary pilgrimage, but the priest assured me that this one would surely bring me comfort, and so I undertook it. I lay down and with my *da* (a large knife used by all the natives of this tribe), marked the place where my head rested. Rising I placed my feet on this mark and lay down again, repeating this process over and over until I reached the shrine. This pilgrimage was quite as useless as the first so far as I was able to judge, and when I once more reached the priest's house he put me in charge of his cows.

CHAPTER VIII.

SERVING A PRIEST FOR ETERNAL LIFE.

"I FOUND my new master very exacting and unmerciful. The more I watched his every-day life the more I was convinced that he was not sinless. One day a company of devotees were bowing down in most abject posture worshipping him, and he gave them assurance, as he had given me, that he could forgive sins because he himself was sinless, when I overheard a company of *dooms* (low caste people) bitterly denouncing the 'Great One of the Earth,' because he had cheated a poor woman out of all her little property, and had also taken possession of a poor man's cow. The widow, they said, had gone to him when her husband died, and begged him to take charge of her pecuniary affairs. He consented, and took so good care of her money that she never saw an *anna* of it herself. (An *anna* is a coin of about three cents value.) The man who lost the cow had gone to the priest to have him reveal the whereabouts of the animal, little dreaming that the wily priest had it in concealment. He paid a good price to have the priest tell him where he could find the cow, but for a wonder that day the priest was not all-wise and could reveal nothing.

"One very hot day while watching the cows as they grazed near the edge of the jungle I fell asleep, and while I slept a huge Bengal tiger carried off one of the cows. I knew the priest would be wild with rage when he came to know of his loss, and I was tempted to run away and leave the rest of the cows to the mercy of the tigers, rather than to encounter his burst of temper. However, my conscience would not allow me to do this, and I drove the herd home and frankly told the priest what had happened. He seized me by the hair, and holding me firmly against a banyan tree, he deliberately rubbed red pepper in my eyes. In vain did I plead for mercy—his eyes glared like those of a savage beast, and he rejoiced over my intense suffering. After this event nothing could induce me to remain longer as a learner of the Hindoo religion. For how could a man so cruel and brutal know anything about the mercy and forgiveness for which I had so long worked and waited? I had heard of a Mohammedan teacher living some miles west of the priest's home, and I made my way to him. When he told me that he did not believe in idol worship, but that the prophet Mohammed was his teacher, and as he had given up five years of his life to holy contemplation in a cave, at the end of which time the angel Gabriel had appeared to him in visions and revelations; surely this one leader must be a safe guide to follow. 'There is but one God, and Mohammed is his Prophet,' devoutly remarked this, my new-found Mussulman teacher. I was rejoiced to hear words from the Koran, for they were more like what a true god might say to me, than all the *slokas* of the Hindoo Shasters. And so I stayed with this teacher three months. Alas! I was obliged to witness the wicked and licentious lives of the followers of Mohammed. I heard the teacher tell them that it is right to steal from those who would not believe as he and they did, and even to murder them in order to advance the Mussulman religion. How could these people help me to find a higher and a better life, when they themselves were worse in their conduct than the Hindoos? And I was convinced that the simple hill people among whom I had been brought up were kinder hearted and lived far better lives than either the Hindoos or Mohammedans. When I reached my home on the mountains I found that my foster-father had long ago left for parts unknown. I sat down on the ground where my mother's *chang* had stood during the days of her funeral, and thought of her as the best example for me to follow, of any I had yet found. I was completely discouraged with the result of my investigations for the truth. That night I slept under the great tree where I had so often made my offerings in the days of my childhood. And I dreamed that a man came to me and said, 'Korno Siga, I have a book for you.' That dream impressed me so forcibly that I went through the village inquiring of every one if he or she could tell me of any one who had a book. They all laughed at me and asked sarcastically, 'and what would a monkey of the forest do with a book?' But I was seriously in earnest in this matter, and went from village to village, everywhere making the inquiry, 'Have you a book?' At length on the outskirts of one of the villages I came upon a man who lived alone in his little hut. He sat in the open door, and ere I had put my question to him, I saw that he held in his hand a book.

"'What book is that?' I eagerly asked; 'is it for me?'

"'Yes, it is for you and for every one. It is the Shaster of the white people.'

"Saying this he opened the book and read, 'God so loved the world, that he gave his only begotten Son, that whosoever believeth in him should not perish, but have everlasting life.' And 'Come unto me, all *ye* that labour and are heavy laden, and I will give you rest.'

"I asked the reader who it was that had spoken such precious words.

"He replied, 'These are the words of Christ, the Saviour of the world. He revealed himself to us by leading a sinless and holy life here in our Orient; he showed us God in human flesh, offered up his own life for us, and has now gone to get mansions ready for his children, *i. e.*, those who obey and love him; and he is coming again to receive us and welcome us to those mansions.'

"I asked him to read over and over again that cordial invitation, until I could repeat the words as Christ had said them.

"Then I begged him to let me have the Shaster for my own, but he said that a hundred rupees could not buy that precious book from him, for he loved it better than his own life. He told me also that his name was Phrang, and that he had been a student in a Christian school, and had been taught by the white teachers. His wife and all of his relatives had forsaken him because he had become a Christian. He was in the village trying to induce other young men to enter that Christian school, and he should return with four such on the morrow. I begged of him a native primer, which had in it some quotations from the Christian Shaster. Many times during that night I arose from my bed and prayed to the primer, hoping that in this way Christ might speak to me through the little book, and tell me how I might come to him and find his promised rest.

"Early the next morning I went again to Phrang's house, hoping that he had not yet started for the mission station. Alas! I found him in the last stages of cholera. He had been attacked during the night and had not been able to call in any one to help him. Indeed, there were few of his friends who would have helped him if they had known of his illness, for was he not in their estimation a Christian dog?

"As I entered the room he pointed to a little bamboo shelf where lay his precious Shaster, and when I handed it to him he clasped it to his heart, and handed it back to me, signifying that it was mine, and raising his hand heavenward, he died. I went in search of the young men who were to have gone with him to the mission school. But when they heard that he had died of cholera, they decided that he must have been a bad man because the cholera god had killed him; and they refused to learn the white man's religion lest they too should be killed. And so I have come alone bringing with me Phrang's Shaster." Saying this he slowly unwrapped the book from many folds of his turban, and asked if he might be allowed to have it for his own. When told that he was now its rightful owner he made his salaam and said: "O teachers of Christ's religion, give me a place among you, that I may learn the truth."

All present were deeply moved at his earnest

plea. One aged man went eagerly forward and lifted Korno Siga's arm and carefully examined it, exclaiming, "This young man is my adopted son, for here on his arm is the mark by which I shall always know him, as my successor to my office as a chief among the hill men." Korno Siga had indeed found his foster-parent, and they were now both seeking the truth as revealed by Christ.

Through what devious ways had they been led during those years of separation! Who of us shall say there is not a divinity that rules over the inhabitants of India as well as of our own fair Columbia?

> "For God through ways they have not known
> Shall lead his own."

CHAPTER IX.

EARTHQUAKES AND WHITE ANTS.

THE two destructive agents to houses and all household goods in Assam are earthquakes and white ants; and I propose in this chapter to tell you something about them.

One Sunday afternoon a large company of our people were gathered in our compound, and we were talking to them of the wonders of nature and the wisdom and love of nature's God.

The Bible lesson for the young men of the Normal School that day had been in the book of Job at the thirty-seventh chapter, and this theme had interested not only them, but also the large number of visitors from the surrounding country.

Suddenly our conversation was interrupted by a death-like stillness which seemed to pervade all things. Not a leaf quivered and the air seemed destitute of all vitality; a stillness so awe-inspiring that dumb creatures as well as human beings gazed helplessly about with a nameless fear. This was followed by a rumbling noise like a heavy freight train in the distance; finally came the majestic quaking of mother Earth. Huge forest trees swayed to and fro and vast sides of the mountain were broken off, and fell with a thundering crash into the valley below. Houses reeled like drunken men, and the ground rose in undulations like sea-waves during a calm. The current in the little river near our bungalow set up stream, and the earth in places opened up and sent forth a strong sulphurous odor. The natives far and near had fled from their houses when the first warning of the earthquake came, and many hundreds gathered in our mission compound, whither we too had gone when the house began to rock. It was ever thus in times of danger with this people of Assam: they would seek protection of the missionary with an inward feeling that the Great Spirit was in sympathy with us, and that they were safer on mission ground than elsewhere.

It soon became impossible for any one to stand, and as we sat upon the ground, each looked at the other wondering what would come next. Our native nurse, Padma, had taken little Ruth into the nursery and was singing a weird lullaby song to her when the earthquake began. We called to her to run with the baby into the compound with us, but when she got as far as the verandah she stood paralyzed with fear, and I was obliged to take the child from her, while Mr. Marston conducted Padma to the bottom of the steps just as they fell. She too fell near a tree and clasping its roots she began praying to the Hindoo gods. And this was the form of her prayer: "O Ram, Krishna, and Shiva, have mercy upon us and make the elephant stop shaking himself!" The Hindoos of Assam believe that the earth is flat, and that it stands on the back of an elephant. He has never given himself a good thorough shaking up since the earth was created; when he does, then the end of all things will come. The present quaking was only a moderate shaking of his head, and all of the little earthquakes are simply a winking of his eyelashes and a tremor of the hair in the centre of his forehead! The last named are used by the native jewellers in India to surround their ornaments of silver filigree work and lend quite a pretty effect to their jewels.

As shock after shock came in quick succession, I began to fear that the final great shaking had indeed come. The goats, cows and ponies were running in frantic alarm from one point of the compass to another, and it was quite frightful to hear their cries of distress. The natives were moaning and praying all about us. Of all the people gathered there, only two were perfectly calm and self-possessed, Mr. Marston and Korno Siga. Mr. Marston said quietly, "We will read from God's word to his children, for he is saying to us now, 'Be still, and know that I *am* God,'" and turning to the ninetieth Psalm, Korno Siga read in clear full tones: "Lord, thou hast been our dwelling-place in all generations. Before the mountains were brought forth, or ever thou hadst formed the earth and the world, even from everlasting to everlasting, thou *art* God."

Thus reassured, the young men of the school and all the converts so far overcame their fears as to join in that grand old hymn, "God moves in a mysterious way," etc.

Christianity seen thus in contrast with the wild and frantic cries of the heathen, convinces the most skeptical that there is a sustaining inherent power in Christianity such as characterizes no other religion.

We could not sleep in our own bungalow that night, but took refuge in a native hut. During the night we had seventeen more shocks, and during the following fortnight we had forty-eight earthquakes, more or less severe. Weeks passed before we dared to disrobe ourselves for a good night's rest; we expected any moment to be obliged to seek the open air for safety. Our little ones asked pleadingly: "Can we never go to bed like white folks any more? Have we turned into natives since the earthquake?" To one who has never experienced the sensations produced by an almost constant tremor of the earth, it is quite impossible for me to describe our feelings during that ever-to-be-remembered fortnight. I often found myself quoting, "If the foundations be destroyed, what can the righteous do?"

But at length the feeling of security came back to us and we resumed our former habits of life, thankful that the "elephant had stopped shaking himself."

Personally, there is nothing that so thoroughly frightens me as an earthquake. I have experienced many perils by land and by sea, but none of them moves me like an earthquake. One of our aged Christian converts used to say, "The Marston Mem Saheb is a brave woman and can face almost any danger, but when an earthquake comes along she can run as fast as anybody." This old man was having prayers at our house one evening and during his prayer an earthquake shook the house severely. When he arose from his knees, he found that his whole audience had run away and left him praying alone!

He did not know the unsafe condition of our house as we did. Every bungalow throughout that whole section of country was more or less in ruins after that severe earthquake, and it required much labor and expense before our house was again a safe retreat. Besides we had lost nearly all of our dishes and glassware and bottled medicines, as our *almirahs* (or cupboards) had all been thrown down and badly demolished.

Our white ants, termites or wood-worms as they

are variously called, are capable of devouring anything except metals and stones. We have in Assam the usual five classes among the termites, viz.: males, females, workers, neuters and soldiers. The males and females also have four long wings nearly equal in length. Eighty thousand is the estimated number of eggs which one female lays in twenty-four hours. The workers are wingless and are by far the most numerous. The neuters have four wing-cases on the thorax. This class waits upon the king and queen and takes care of the young ants. The soldiers are similar in appearance to the neuters, but are more fully developed and have very large jaws, and are the military force of the white ant tribe.

The houses built by the termites are of great size and have long spiral passages connecting with a subterranean abode. Their cones are often ten or twelve feet high, relatively as large for them as buildings five times the height of the Egyptian pyramids would be for human beings, and are built of earth which has been softened in the jaws of the workers. This quickly dries and forms a most substantial ant structure. Their habitations abound everywhere in the jungles, and every available article which is consumable falls a prey to these destructive creatures. They will devour any soft wood tree, root and branch. They are quite as industrious as the bee and quickly rebuild their structures if they are allowed to do so. Snakes and birds devour these ants with a relish, and the natives consider them quite a dainty dish after they have been roasted. When our rainy season is about setting in, we often see myriads of the winged ants filling the air, but most of them are destroyed when the rain commences. The workers are always on the lookout at this time for a king and queen, and if a pair of these winged or perfect ants escape death from the waters, they become henceforth the royal pair and the founders of a new colony. It is exceedingly interesting to watch the founding of a colony of white ants. There are many chambers and galleries in their houses. In one, the queen is imprisoned, where she is waited upon by numerous neuters whose apartments open from the queen's. These attendants carry off the eggs as soon as they are laid, and for this alone eighty thousand trips are required in twenty-four hours. The eggs are stored in rooms, and when the young ants are hatched the neuters take care of them. There are various perforated passages leading to the nurseries, store-rooms, ground-floor and underground entrances. The pregnant female is five inches long and two-thirds of an inch wide, *i. e.*, she is very many times as large as the workers. (See note, p. 87.) The bite of the soldiers is severe and painful and much dreaded by residents in Assam. These insects are fearfully destructive to our houses and furniture, and they will secretly eat out the interior of the legs of our furniture and the posts of our houses until nothing but a shell is left. They also devour clothing of all kinds. During the first year of our sojourn in the country we stored our clothing for the cold season in large trunks and boxes which were not tin-lined; and when we came to examine them we found not a vestige of anything that we could recognize. A few scraps of blankets and cloaks were left, but were so covered over with the new earth and saliva of these white ants that we could recognize neither color nor texture. We resolved that we would ferret out their habitations and miserably destroy their city. After digging twenty feet in the ground we came upon her royal majesty, the queen of the colony. She was an ugly white worm five inches or more long, and bore no resemblance to her numerous progeny except in the shape of the head and fore-legs. After killing her the colony rapidly dispersed and doubtless went off to join themselves to some other queen. I need not add that we did not go into mourning over the queen and the dispersion of her subjects.

It is not an unusual thing for a piece of furniture which has all the outward appearance of solidity suddenly to sink to the floor, and upon examination prove to be nothing but a thin shell from which the whole interior has been gnawed out by these termites.* Houses fall in the same way, unless we select the very hardest of wood for the posts. In Assam we use the hal, or the teak-wood for posts, all other kinds being too soft. The natives use the bamboo for their little huts; this is a hard wood, but not large enough for the European houses.

* "The Termitidæ are almost all inhabitants of the tropics, only a few comparatively small species being found in temperate climates. These species occur in southern Europe, one of which (*Termes lucifugus*) is abundant in some parts of France. . . . Another (*T. flavicollis*) is a North African species, . . . and the third (*T. flavipes*) appears to have been introduced from South America." They are found in Jamaica, and a ground-living species, the celebrated *Termes bellicosus*, of South Africa, are very destructive.

In the egg-laying season the eggs are developed in such enormous numbers that the abdomen of the insect becomes quite helpless, merely consuming food and producing eggs. See Prof. P. M. Duncan's "Natural History," Vol. VI., pp. 136–138.

CHAPTER X.

AN ASSAMESE FAIRY TALE.

PADMA, our children's nurse, whose name, by the way, means a lily, though she was the blackest lily I ever saw, was never weary of telling fairy tales. Some of them were very foolish and hardly worth writing out for the children of a civilized country, as they had to do mostly with the exploits of the million of gods and goddesses of the Hindoos. We always insisted upon hearing these stories ourselves before our children should be regaled by them, as we well knew that the Hindoo children were told most frightful stories in order to make them go quietly to bed. I have often heard a Hindoo mother tell her child, that if it opened its mouth to say another word, a jackal or a tiger would eat it up at once.

The following fairy tale is one of her best, and its lesson is good enough for children of every land.

Ram Singh was a very selfish boy, who would always take the best of everything for himself. Early in life he decided that he would live for himself alone and never do anything to help another person, whatever the need might be. He worked very hard indeed, but his labor was all for himself, and the more he toiled the poorer he grew. At the age of forty he found himself with a wife and twelve children, and not a single rupee, anna, nor pice to buy food and clothes for them. "The gods are unjust," he said, "and I will go to the wise man of the temple and learn my fate." And so he made his way through the dense jungle filled with wild beasts, to the temple where the wise man lived. On the road he met a camel with two sacks of treasure on his back. The poor animal seemed utterly exhausted, and leaned heavily against a rubber tree to rest. He had been wandering twelve years, having been lost from a caravan, and during all these years had found no one to direct him.

"Where are you going?" asked the camel.

"To seek my fate," the selfish man replied.

"Ask mine too," begged the camel. "Woe is me."

Then the selfish man travels on until he comes to a great river in which is a crocodile.

"Take me over the river," said the man.

"I will," said the crocodile, "but first tell me whither you are going."

"The gods have been cruel and unjust to me, and I go to the temple to ask why my fate is so hard, and I so very, very poor."

"Ask my fate too, for I have had a burning pain in my stomach for twelve years, and I can get no relief. Woe is me," moaned the crocodile.

"I will ask your fate too," said the man, and he hurried on.

And as he journeyed on he came to a tiger, a royal Bengal man-eater, lying in the thicket in great pain, and there were precious stones and rare treasures strewed all about him, which had belonged to the man he had eaten.

"Where are you going?"

"To the temple of fate, to talk with the wise man."

"Ask my fate too, for I have had this thorn in my foot for twelve years, and I can find no comfort or help anywhere. Woe is me."

"I will," answered the selfish man as he started on to the temple of fate.

There the wise old man asked him, "What seek you here?"

"I seek my fate. I have a poor wife and twelve poverty-stricken children, and I am very, very poor."

"Then you must have been living for yourself all these years. Go home and think only of making others rich, and you will surely become rich yourself."

Then he asked the fate of the poor camel.

"Take the sacks off his back, and both of you will be relieved. Why did you not do it before?"

"I was thinking only of myself."

Then he asked the fate of the crocodile.

"Give him herb tea, and both of you will be relieved. Why did you not do it before?"

"I was thinking only of myself."

"And what shall be the fate of the tiger?"

"Take the thorn out of his foot, and both of you will be relieved."

The man returned, took the thorn from the tiger's foot, and as compensation received all of the precious stones and treasures which were strewn about him. He gathered herbs and made a tea, and gave to the crocodile for the pain in his stomach. The crocodile threw up the tea, and along with it a diamond of priceless value, the celebrated diamond of India, and this became the property of the once selfish man. He lifted the two sacks from the camel's back, and they also were bestowed upon him. And the poor man went back to his family a rich man, for he that helps others is sure to be helped himself.

CHAPTER XI.

KORNO SIGA AS A STUDENT.

NEVER have missionaries welcomed to their school a more earnest, persevering student than Korno Siga proved to be. After he had learned all he could about his own language, he set about the ancient Sanscrit, which is the classical language of India. He learned to read the Hindoo Shasters in that language, that he might better compare them with the Christian Bible. Often I have gone during the small hours of the night and found him still poring over his books, and when I begged him to put them aside and go to bed, he would reply, "let me follow out this subject a little further, for it is more interesting to me than any other on earth." He wrote out a long list of moral sayings of the Shasters, and opposite each he placed the infinitely higher moral precepts of the Bible. He wrote out also the history of Krishna, the Hindoo incarnation who is claimed to be one and the same as Christ.

Korno Siga also made a careful study of the Koran and Mohammedanism as he saw it exemplified in the lives of the Mussulmans about him.

He made frequent trips to his native village, and returning brought other young men with him from the hill tribes to enter the Normal School. This school was now well established, and was generously aided by the English government. During the second year of Korno Siga's stay in the school he was attacked with cholera, that scourge of India, which finds its origin in the valley of the Ganges, and from thence spreads over all India. Henry and I did all that human care and kindness could accomplish for him. Our knowledge of medicine was considerable, and we were exceed ingly anxious that it should be effectual with our beloved mountain chief. He suffered intensely from the contraction of the muscles and could only get relief by being most thoroughly rubbed with stimulating liniment. After giving him freely of "Squibb's Cholera Medicine," which every missionary ought to be supplied with in India, we succeeded in checking the disease. But having lost so much of the watery portion of the blood we feared that he could not rally. Hence we gave him copious drinks of salt water, and when he was threatened with collapse we gave large doses of calomel. We did not then know of the tannic acid treatment.

After his recovery he was so grateful that he seemed unable to do enough for us. He realized that his life had been spared that he might be useful to his countrymen, and he finally decided that he ought to come out boldly and confess his allegiance to Christ's religion, and the day was appointed for his baptism.

The evening previous to that day he came to me and asked if he could talk with me alone. "You are a mother, and perhaps you can understand what I shall now tell you better than any one else. I have been thinking a great deal lately about my foster-mother. She was a good woman, and I believe that she lived just as near right as she knew how. She taught me to be truthful, honest, and kind, and I am sure that if she had heard of the Christian religion, she would have believed in it. But she never had an opportunity of hearing one word about Christ. If she has gone to the place of unhappiness and punishment, I think I ought to go there also and try to make her as comfortable as possible! It would be very selfish of me, to enter eternal bliss and leave her alone in eternal woe. Hence I have decided not to be baptized, nor be a Christian, so that I may go to her and help her all I can."

"My dear brother," I replied, "do you suppose our kind Heavenly Father would ever treat your foster-mother unjustly? Eternal wretchedness after death arises from a sense of sin committed during life and a consequent remorse of conscience. If your mother lived up to all the light she had and kept the whole law, how could she suffer from remorse? You must leave the future condition of your mother in the hands of One who is too wise to err and too good to be unkind. 'He will order all events so that you will be abundantly satisfied.' The Apostle Peter said to Cornelius and his company: 'Of a truth I perceive that God is no respecter of persons, but in every nation he that feareth him, and worketh righteousness, is accepted with him,' and then he declares to these seekers after the truth, Christ and the remission of sins."

I assured Korno Siga, moreover, that with the instruction and additional light which he had received, if he should refuse the Saviour and his proffered atonement he would be far more subject to punishment than his good foster-mother. And so on the following day he was baptized and was one of the most joyful of converts. He was the first of his tribe baptized by my husband, and we hoped for great usefulness from his faithful work among his people. Personally, I will add that I have never known a heathen who lived up to all the light he had received. Who has?

The Normal School opened at ten o'clock every morning, excepting Sunday. The opening exercises consisted of reading of the Scriptures in the native language, a careful exposition of the truth read, and questioning with reference to the lesson of the preceding day. Then all bowed in prayer while my husband led them audibly. The young men were all very fond of music and were never tired of singing our sweet Christian hymns. Geography, arithmetic, grammar and history were the studies usually pursued during the ordinary three years' course.

But the people of Assam are naturally a religious people, and much of the time was spent in studying Christianity as compared with Vedaism, Brahmanism and Hindooism. This last named religion like Buddhism is a protest against Brahmanism, but differs from Buddhism in that it is theistic, while Buddhism says, "There is no God: the hope of humanity is in itself."

"The Indian mind," says Leighton Parks, in his 'Star in the East,' "has always shrunk from materialism, because it leads to atheism; Hindooism is saturated with theism." It is impossible for the Hindoo mind to see any beauty in annihilation, and the question is ever being asked, "If a man die, shall he live *again?*"

Korno Siga, although a mountaineer, was intensely interested in the study of the religions of the world, and the more he studied, the more firmly rooted was he in the belief that God had not left himself without witness among the nations of the earth; and when a group of hill men or of Hindoos came to talk with him, he was very fond of taking for his text, "The unknown god. Whom therefore ye ignorantly worship, him declare I unto you." And the secret of his success in leading his countrymen into the light was the deep religious experience he had himself undergone in coming to that light "which lighteth every man that cometh into the world." If we would win souls to Christ we must ever follow his methods of work, and with an infinite love and pity put ourselves in the place of the ignorant and benighted, and reason with them from their own standpoint. Lyman Abbott beautifully expresses this thought: "The missionary movement is not merely a philanthropic movement; it does not derive its power from a mere sentiment of pity for men and fear for their future. Its inspiration lies in a spiritual sense of what it is for a child of God to live in ignorance of his Father and in isolation from him, and in the hopefulness caught from faith in and communion with a God whose faith in the possibilities of man and whose hope for and love towards him are infinite and inexhaustible. As the church has studied the life and character of Christ it has caught his spirit; it has imbibed his life and followed his example."

CHAPTER XII.

KORNO SIGA'S BRIDE.

AMONG the girls who had come to me from the hills for instruction was a bright, pretty one whom we called Kache. She was from one of the remote villages of Korno Siga's tribe, and was of an independent family who had never been slaves.

When the Burmese invaded Assam, there were certain families among the hill tribes who rendered such valuable service to the Assamese army, that they and their descendants were made forever exempt from slavery. As a sign of their independence a blue line of India ink was traced from the vertex of the frontal bone to the bottom of the chin. Since 1826, when the English government took possession of the country, the slavery system has been abolished, and the blue line only tells the story of former cruelty and barbarism. But the descendants of these independent families still retain the blue line. Kache had the blue line most clearly drawn upon her face, but she certainly bore no other mark of aristocracy. Her hair had never known the comb nor brush; indeed she had never seen a comb. Her fingers had always served her in that line, so far as keeping rubbish and twigs out of her hair was concerned. Her clothing was meagre and filthy, when she put in her appearance at the mission bungalow. She had travelled in company with an old woman of her tribe, and their journey had been through dense jungles infested with wild animals. She had heard of my school for girls through one of Mr. Marston's preaching tours on the hills. He had spent two days at Kache's village, and had told the people of our desire to have them educated and christianized. He had urged the parents to send their girls to school as well as their boys, that they too might know a better life than the mere animal existence which was then theirs.

Kache listened to the strange words of the white man, as she stood behind one of the little bamboo huts, and she rejoiced to hear that there was a religion which recognized the worth of woman, and permitted her to learn from the sacred books. She resolved that she would some day seek the missionary's school, and learn to be something more than a wild animal of the jungle. The journey from her home to our mission station required eleven days, and the road was only a footpath through the dense jungle.

At night she and the old woman were obliged to climb the trees, and tie themselves to the limbs, lest they should fall while asleep, and be devoured by the ravenous beasts of prey. All night long the Bengal tigers roared, the jackals howled, and the bears growled in the forest about them. When the morning light came, however, they hied themselves away to their lairs in the depths of the jungle. There are no hotels in that wild country, and Kache must needs carry with her, her mat for her bed, and dishes in which to cook her rice and *dahl* (split peas). And thus through many hardships and dangers did she reach the mission station and the bungalow of the missionary. I was seated on the broad verandah which surrounded our bungalow, when she came up the steps and announced herself in this fashion: "I have come to learn to be somebody." The filthiest of all filthy creatures, with vermin creeping over her, she certainly looked as though she was quite a nobody. Seating herself upon the verandah floor (what did she know of chairs?) she commenced shaking out her coarse black hair, while ever and anon she would seize a piece of cotton, a leaf, stick or one of the vermin, and fling it from her.

Changing my position so that I might not come within range of her missiles, I asked: "And you wish to be somebody, do you? What do you mean by that?"

"I want to learn to read and write, and become a white Christian."

"Cleanliness is next to godliness, and if you want to be a white Christian, the first thing for you to do, is to bathe and put on clean garments. When you have done that we will talk about your being somebody."

But Kache most vehemently protested against making so complete a change in her personal appearance. "I cannot bathe; neither my mother, grandmother, nor any of my ancestors ever did such a thing; and how can I depart from the customs of my forefathers?"

I assured her that I should never receive her into the school unless she complied with these requirements. I threw open the door of the school-room and showed her my neat-looking class of girls who had come to me looking just as she looked; and soap, water, and clean clothes had wrought the difference, I assured her.

"If I should go back to my village looking as they do, every one would make sport of me and drive me out of the place. Besides I did not come all this long way to hear such words as you speak. I came to hear about the white man's religion. May I not sit on the verandah every day, and listen as you teach the people who come to you each day?"

I assured her that she might do this even though she was so filthy, but that she must not enter the school. Day after day she came and sat with the village people and listened to the words of Jesus, that oriental Teacher who taught as never man taught; but she still strongly refused to bathe or put on the clean clothes which I had in readiness for her.

One day she came to the bungalow and as I was not on the verandah to meet her, she made her way to my dressing-room. Facing the door of the room was a large mirror, and when Kache saw her image reflected there she started back and seemed much frightened.

"What wild beast do you keep in that place?" she asked, looking towards the mirror.

I assured her that there were no wild beasts about our house—that she was looking into a mirror which showed her just what she looked like. I asked her if she had not often seen her image in the water.

She said she had, but it did not look half so frightful as that creature in the mirror.

I told her if she would take the bath and put on clean clothes, she could quite materially improve "the creature in the mirror;" that wild animals of the jungle looked better than she, for they are clean. I urged the matter upon her in the strongest of terms, assuring her that she would always be glad she took the step after once the decision was made. After much argument and hesitation, she made the decision I so ardently hoped for, and went to the little river near our house for her bath. An old Hindoo woman who had become a Christian went with her, and after the bath, she cut Kache's hair and combed it for her. It was utterly impossible to get a comb through it, on account of the accumulated debris of years. In a couple of hours Kache returned to the house clad in her clean white garments; her hair had been wet in mustard oil, after the custom of the Assamese Hindoo women, and plastered tight to her head. She was so entirely transformed that I wished her to see herself again in the looking-glass, and I led her to the dressing-room, and bade her look once more upon the wild creature she had feared. She was more than pleased with the apparition before her, and with a broad grin exclaimed, "How pretty I am now! Surely I am a Christian, for I am clean."

I tried to explain to her the difference between physical cleanliness and soul purity, and told her that she could never be a true Christian until she had received as thorough a cleansing of her heart, as she had just had of her body; that the Bible and God's Holy Spirit could show her the condition of her heart more thoroughly than the mirror and the sunlight had shown her physical uncleanness. "The Christian religion makes one clean inside as well as outside, and the soul soiled with sin must be washed in that fountain which

Christ has opened for sin, and must put on a robe of Christ's righteousness before one can be a true Christian." Kache did not comprehend all these words at that time. She entered the school the next day and showed an eager desire for a knowledge of books, and was a most persevering student. When she had been only four months in the school, one Sunday morning she heard a sermon which Mr. Marston preached from the text, "If any man *be* in Christ, *he is* a new creature," etc. This sermon made a deep impression upon her, and during the afternoon she came to me and asked me to explain it to her more fully. I reminded her of her looking-glass experience, and how little she realized her need of a bath until she caught one good view of herself. "God's word of truth is the looking-glass of the soul, and you have had a view of your spiritual condition in that looking-glass this morning, and when one sees the need of a heavenly cleansing, the Bible points to the fountain of Christ's righteousness and says, 'Wash ye, make you clean.'" Is. 1 : 16.

"But where is that fountain, and who will take me to it?" she eagerly asked. Long and patiently did I talk to her during the hours of that Sunday afternoon, of him who is the Way, the Truth and the Life; of his divine power to generate in the sinful heart a new and holy purpose; of that wisdom which comes from above and is known only by those who are obedient to the heavenly vision. Christ himself has plainly said to us, that if we will do his will we shall know of the doctrine. No wonder that so many grope in darkness, and wander into materialism and agnosticism, when they try, by their own weak reason, to find out a truth which can only be known by obedience. At length Kache seemed to catch a glimpse of Christ's mercy and loving kindness, and asked me to pray with her that she might be an obedient child of this wise and loving Friend.

"What does he want me to do first for him?"

"You have repented of all your past sins; you believe his holy word—that word says 'believe and be baptized.' Baptism is the public sign by which you say to the world that your heart has had the baptism in the Holy Spirit. Is not this your first step?"

That evening, as our little band of Christians met for prayer, Kache told them of her experience, and how she believed that she was now a new creature in Christ. One old deacon in the church who believed in bodily suffering and penance for sin, and who had absorbed a great deal of Hindooism into his Christianity, asked Kache if she had spent three days and three nights wrestling in agony for her forgiveness, and he assured her that unless she had spent as long a time at least as Jonah was in the whale's belly, she could not be a

Christian. Mr. Marston and I were obliged to laugh heartily at this novel statement, and Mr. Marston asked the old man if his father kept him three days and three nights in torture, before he would forgive his boyish disobedience. "Carlyle says, 'repentance is the noblest emotion of which a human being is capable,'" said my husband; "and is our God a vindictive being who delights in torturing his children? No, no, he is like a kind, loving, forgiving parent, who is delighted to forgive an erring child and receive him into the fullest confidence." When Kache made her public espousal of the Christian religion, a glow of heavenly peace and joy shone in her face, as one after another of the native church members gathered about her to welcome her to their Christian brotherhood.

Korno Siga was among this number, and I observed that he welcomed her a little more cordially than the others, with which fact I was well pleased, though I kept my thoughts to myself. The morning after her baptism, Kache came to me and asked if she might start for her native village that day, as she was in a hurry to tell her parents and friends of this "wonderful religion which makes one clean outside and inside." I gave my consent for her to go in company with the same old woman who came with her, and who had been helping me in the care of household matters during the time Kache had been in school. Korno Siga objected to the two women going alone, and was on the point of offering to go himself, when I anticipated him and appointed Rong Bong and his wife to go with them. Kache took her Bible and hymn-book with her, and faithfully did she use them during the weeks she remained in her native village. Great was the surprise of the villagers at her changed personal appearance, and greatly did they wonder at the new strange words she spake to them. She told them how she had learned of Christ, and urged them also to be obedient to this divine preacher who had become her personal Saviour. So great was her influence among her people that she persuaded a number of the other girls of her village to accompany her when she returned to the school. In this school they not only learned of the Christian religion, but were taught all of the common branches of knowledge, and were trained in housekeeping and needle-work. About a year after her visit to her native village, Korno Siga came to me, and begged that she might be given to him in marriage. I asked him how he knew she loved him and would marry him.

"Oh, I know she loves me; for she always blushes and looks down when I offer her the betel nut." The next time I met Kache, I asked her what she thought of Korno Siga as a teacher among her people; would they like him, and would he be useful among them if I should send him to live among them? Kache's manner told the whole story, and I gave permission to Korno Siga to wed her. They went after their marriage and lived in Kache's village, and spent their time in teaching the ignorant people knowledge, useful and practical. Above all, the good tidings of salvation and an immortality beyond the grave was the theme of their constant conversation, and much good did they accomplish by their faithful work.

CHAPTER XIII.

SNAKE-CHARMERS AND ROYAL BENGAL TIGERS.

THE boa is the largest and most powerful of the serpents of Assam. Some of these serpents are thirty feet in length, and can masticate and swallow a buffalo. They first crush the bones thoroughly and then covering them with saliva they lengthen the carcass until it is small enough for them to swallow. Frequently in our travels through the jungles, did we come within hearing of the agonizing cries of some poor beast which was being crushed to death by the coils of this powerful serpent. When the beast is large, the boa contrives to get it between himself and a tree and thus more readily crushes it into swallowing dimensions. Occasionally a human being is caught in the coils of the serpent as he is taking his bath in the river. The boa winds his tail about a tree growing at the water's edge, and thus floats out to his unsuspecting victim.

The following snake-story was told me by a native who solemnly assured me that it was true in every detail. Two men and a woman were travelling through the jungle, and as the universal custom in Assam is for the woman to follow in the rear, she was the one to fall into the coils of the boa who lay coiled near their path. She, as most women would have done under like circumstances, set up most vigorous feminine screeches. The men told her to keep quiet and they would rescue her, and one of them who carried a coop of young pigeons at once offered one to the serpent which greedily devoured it. Another and another were given in quick succession; meanwhile the second man had made his way with all speed to the bazaar where he bought two hundred more pigeons, and they continued to feed the boa until the third day after he had embraced the woman. By this time he was thoroughly gorged and releasing his hold of the woman fell to the ground and was quickly despatched by the natives, who had assembled for this purpose with immense clubs and other implements of death. Perhaps this is too big a snake-story to believe, but a native policeman told it to me and I repeat it to you.

There are many water snakes in Assam, and some of them are very venomous. One night, when travelling by boat, I lifted my pillow to place my bunch of keys underneath it, and found a huge snake coiled there against which my hand struck. He quickly slid away and I could nowhere find him, and I was under the necessity of retiring without knowing his whereabouts, though he had doubtless found his way into the river. I was not then as intimately acquainted with the snake family as I have since become, and must confess to a feminine nervousness which somewhat interrupted my slumbers. I dare say this form of nervousness dates back to that affair in the garden of Eden, when mother Eve met a snake and was worsted in the encounter.

The russclean and the whip-snake are both venomous and are quite common in Assam. But the most fatally poisonous is the cobra de capello, or hooded snake. It frequently makes its way into houses, and many natives die annually from its bite. More than once have I heard a thud on my floor at night, and found it was caused by the falling of a cobra from the thatch-covered roof, and I have found its slough two or three times under my children's bed.

One night a terrific storm coming up suddenly, I hastened to close the doors and windows which had been left open on account of the stifling heat. As I entered the bath-room I heard the hiss of the cobra, and hastily sprang backward and went in search of a lamp. On returning I found a large cobra with uplifted trunk and widespread hood confronting me. I called in the *chokedar* (night watchman) and we soon succeeded in killing the snake. We found on closer examination that he had swallowed a toad, and this had made him less agile than usual, and hence he had not struck me with his fangs when I entered the bath-room. Thus my life was saved by a toad.

The Indian jugglers make various uses of this snake, in the wonderful feats with which they astonish the uninitiated. We had not been long in Assam before we were visited by the snake-charmers. Two of these men came to our door and very kindly informed us that the Hindoo gods had told them that our premises were infested by cobras; and moreover, as they were the brothers of the cobra and servants of the gods, they had only to call their brothers and they would come to them.

Mr. Marston replied, "Very well; I will give you a rupee for every cobra you catch for me on my premises."

The charmers took their bamboo fifes and played several weird airs, which made me feel that all the minor strains were concentrated in the fife and in those airs. Then ceasing their music they said in a sing-song tone, "Come, my brother of the jungle, hasten to me; I wait for you; I woo you with my music; I call you with my voice. Come, my brother of the jungle, come."

Very soon a large cobra came gliding from the edge of the grass, and lifting his head he seems to keep time to the music of the fife. He makes his way to the musician and is caught in the hands of the charmer. The snake strikes angrily at the man's hand, and blood seems to flow freely from the wound. The charmer takes a little box of medicine from his girdle and rubs some of it on the wound, and, wiping away the blood, says, "The gods do not permit me to be poisoned by my brother." This performance is repeated until four large cobras are caught, and safely stored in the charmer's baskets. Then the two men came forward to the verandah where we were seated, and making a low salaam asked Mr. Marston for the money.

"Give me my snakes and I will at once pay you for them," is the answer.

To this arrangement the charmers are much opposed, and rather than give up the snakes they turn away from the house without their money.

I need scarcely explain this proceeding by telling you that they were trained snakes whose fangs had been extracted, and the charmers had only a few moments before let them out of their baskets that they might make money by again catching them. The blood which seemed to come on the man's hand was Indian vermilion, which was concealed in a little bag in his hand. I have seen a juggler apparently thrust a knife through the palm of his hand and the blood flow most profusely. He will wipe it thoroughly, and show the hand without a scratch or wound of any kind. The knife was made with a spring which would allow the blade

8

to sink back into the handle, and press upon a bag of vermilion in such a manner as to cause the appearance of a stream of blood flowing over the hand. In the sleeve of his garment he had another blade, shorter by the width of his hand than the one attached to the knife, which he at once glued to the back of his hand, and in this adroit manner deceived the lookers-on.

The cobra is of brownish-yellow color from three to four feet in length. People err who think it a large, powerful snake. It is feared on account of its venom and not for its strength. Its bite is not always fatal. We have had an opportunity of testing pretty thoroughly the various antidotes for the bite of the cobra. Our plan finally adopted was to ligate and cauterize at once, at the same time administering repeatedly large doses of whiskey and small doses of ammonia. The famous Tanjore pills, which contain each about one-fifteenth grain of arsenious acid, are also very efficacious in treating cobra poisoning. This pill is also much used in the malarial fevers of India, and is very happily named, as far as the Assamese are concerned, "*tan*," meaning severe, and "*jor*," a fever. The name is, however, derived from the district in the Madras Presidency which bears this name. The one other remedy which has been conceived to be effectual is Bibron's remedy, but in order for this or the Tanjore pills to reach the case, it must be administered immediately after the bite, as the poisoning is very rapidly introduced into the blood.

Many hundreds of the natives of Assam die annually from the effect of serpent poisoning. The mongoose is erroneously supposed by some to be proof against the poison, and Europeans in India often keep one of these little animals about the premises to destroy the cobras. The fact with reference to this matter is, that the mongoose is so very agile that it can destroy the cobra before it can bite him, by seizing it by the back of the neck and destroying it instantly. The cobra has been known to live seven months without food.

Adders were one of my greatest causes of anxiety in Assam, as some of them are of the exact color of the trees and shrubs, upon the limbs of which they are partial to basking themselves in the sunshine. And as my children were playing in the garden, the nurse has several times been startled by the sight of an adder stretching out its head from a limb towards the children. A lady friend of mine, on taking down a dress from her wardrobe, found an adder in the sleeve of it as she was putting it on. But she escaped unharmed.

The most exciting of all sports in Assam, both among the natives and Europeans, is the hunting of the tiger. The royal Bengal tiger is found in all the jungles, and fearlessly prowls about our houses at night seeking its prey. The man-eater is never satisfied with anything but human flesh; but the other tigers are content with goats, deer, cows and ponies. The native mode of hunting the tiger is to surround him in his lair during the period of day when he is most drowsy, and with very long-handled spears pierce his body through and through from every direction, leaving him no possible chance of escape.

A company of natives came to our bungalow on an average of twice a week to secure Mr. Marston's assistance in destroying these powerful creatures. In a village near us a man-eater destroyed, in one week, three human beings, and the natives were unable to find his hiding-place for the daytime. They entreated Mr. Marston to go with them and put a ball from his trusty rifle into the tiger. This rifle had three separate barrels: one was used for small game and carried shot; the second was for medium-sized animals, such as deer, jackals, leopards and wild hogs; the third carried an immense bullet for tigers, buffaloes and crocodiles.

Mr. Marston mounted his elephant and started for the village. After a most careful search for traces of the tiger's lair they tracked him to a sugar-cane patch about a quarter of a mile from the village. Mr. Marston ordered the natives to thrust in their long spears from three directions, and drive the man-eater from his bed, while he would take charge of his exit from the side whence no native spears were obstructing the way. Mr. Marston remained seated on the elephant; this animal apparently as much interested in the sport as was the Saheb himself. Korno Siga and two others of our Christian people were also on the back of the elephant, and Korno Siga had carried a shot-gun, remarking, " it will make a noise at any rate." I quote from Mr. Marston's account of the shooting:

"As soon as we arrived at the location of the tiger, the natives poked vigorously here and there through the sugar-cane stalks, which were thickly matted together in places, affording a good lair for the ugly beast. At length the monster was disturbed, and made a tremendous leap towards us and our faithful elephant. As soon as his eye caught sight of me and my gun, he seemed to realize that a desperate struggle must be made for his life, and crouching for another leap, which would bring him upon the back of our elephant, his eyes glared like balls of fire, and his countenance had an expression of all vindictive and demoniacal emotions combined. I knew only too well that my life depended upon my rifle, and lifting an earnest prayer that the ball might be directed by an unerring wisdom, I aimed at the frontal bone of the monster's skull. With a terrible roar, which quite put at discount Korno Siga's report from his shot-gun, the cavernous depths of the huge beast seemed quite exhausted, and he rolled over on his side and was dead. We examined the skull, and found the hole where the bullet had penetrated deep into the brain substance. He was the largest of royal Bengal tigers, a magnificent fellow, measuring eleven feet from the nose to the tip of the tail, his body being eight feet long. I hired ten natives to carry him to our bungalow, that the children and Mildred might see the fruit of my spoils. They tied his feet to long bamboo poles, and swung him from these poles as they bore him on their shoulders. The natives came from all the country round about to rejoice over the death of the man-eater. His skull I am keeping to carry home to my father, and his skin makes a royal rug for our drawing-room. I am sure the Lord steadied my nerves to make that splendid shot. Henceforth the natives will look upon me as a blessing to their country: they can appreciate such help as this better than the good they may get from a sermon.

"Speaking of sermons, let me tell you a story of one of our American missionaries who was in great haste to preach a sermon of the typical sort to the natives. He did not know the language at all accurately, but he had a ravenous zeal to do good. After announcing his text, he attempted to tell them that he would open up the subject before his audience in three parts or headings. The word for part or portion in the Assamese language is 'Bhag,' and the word for tiger is 'Bagh.' Our good preacher clearly, and in a most preacher-like tone, told the native audience that he should let loose or open up before them three tigers, and then he went on to enlarge about those tigers; and when he came to the time when he wished to dismiss the congregation, he used the word 'Khedai,' instead of 'Bidai,' and so said he would drive them all out. One of the natives told me that he did not know at all why he should come to this country to let loose tigers, and drive the people out of church. Zeal is a good thing, but zeal and knowledge should always go together.

"Korno Siga and I were out upon a jungle tour yesterday, and came suddenly upon a solitary wild buffalo. He had been driven away from the herd, and was fury itself infuriated. As soon as he saw us he pawed the ground, and tossed the grass and dirt upon his long horns and started for us. There was not a tree within sight for us to climb, and we saw no means of escape from the dreaded animal. It is not a pleasant thought that you may be tossed and gored by an animal like the buffalo, whose horns each measure five feet in length, and hence we ran our level best, and I prayed as I ran, and ran fast as I prayed, but knew not where I was going, whether into greater danger or to a place of safety. The angry beast was so near me at times that I fancied I felt his hot breath on my shoulders, and feared that in spite of all my praying and running I should fall a victim to buffalo fury, when suddenly I came to the bank of a small stream. Korno Siga and I both leaped at once down the steep bank, and found ourselves resting on a projection of rock some five feet above the water edge. We crept down and found that we were safely covered from the sight of the buffalo, whose bellowing and angry pawing we could still hear on the banks above us. This was indeed finding 'the shadow of a great rock in a weary land.'

"A native boat coming along shortly, took us on board, and we reached home in safety. Travelling by boat in this country is a snail-like process. The native rowers are very inert, and insist upon taking their own time, never minding what may be our haste. A native is never in a hurry. As we crawl along the banks of a stream skirted by dense overhanging jungle, which teems with wild buffaloes, elephants, tigers and the rhinoceros (one horned)—the stream itself abounding with hungry crocodiles—compelled as we are to sleep in a dug-out moored to such a shore with only the protection of a bamboo mat: our surroundings are not well fitted to induce calmness of mind and blissful repose. But we get used to it after a while, and after these years of residence in Assam, we can say that no real harm has ever come to us. To the true sportsman this kind of a life is apropos, and I who so intensely enjoyed sporting in my youthful days should not complain of my many opportunities for exhibiting my skill as a marksman. Yet there are times when there comes an element of unpleasantness even in hunting for the royal Bengal tigers and buffaloes.

"Yet, as a missionary doing earnest work for these, my beloved people, I am always happy, and with my priceless rifle and a hatchet at my pillow, and the Lord of all the earth ever with me, I feel but little fear. And I am truly thankful to be doing a work that, but for me, would never be done. My life is counting for more here than it could possibly count for in my native land. Hence, I will gladly spend and be spent for the good of others."

CHAPTER XIV.

KORNO SIGA BECOMES A CHIEF.

WHILE Korno Siga and Kache were thus usefully laboring among their people, Sar Po, the venerable father of Korno Siga and chief of his tribe, was attacked with small-pox and died. According to the laws of the hill tribes, Korno Siga, who previous to this had been a nominal chief, became acting chief in his stead, as this foster-parent had no children of his own. In vain did the missionaries and native Christians urge that the old chief, who in his heart was a believer in Christianity, should be given Christian burial. The heathen were in the majority and their opinion prevailed. And Sar Po's corpse was placed on the bamboo *chang*, and a little roof built over it to protect it from the vultures and jackals. Mourners were hired to weep and wail, and beat their chests, and tear their hair for fifteen days, during which time the spirit of the dead man was supposed to be seeking an abode. But when the fifteen days were over, the people feasted and danced for yet fifteen days more, because they believed the spirit had found a resting place. At the end of the thirty days the corpse was covered with pitch and straw, and cremated, the ashes being carefully gathered up and kept in a memorial urn that future generations might look upon them and remember the chief, Sar Po.

Though Korno Siga was now chief, he was none the less interested in the Christianization of his people, and he was able to wield a wider influence for good than before. One day when he had gone to look after some of the business interests of his tribe with an adjoining tribe, he sat down under a hal tree to eat his rice, and a landholder of considerable note came and talked with him, asking him many questions about his tribe, his religion, and his business interests. Korno Siga, always on the lookout for benefiting the people, took his Testament and read from it some of the words of Jesus. The man, whose name was Habe, listened with much interest, and asked for a tract as Korno Siga left. The tract was a portion of the gospels of the New Testament, and Habe, who had learned to read in a Hindoo school, read it closely while he kept it concealed for six months. At the end of that time he very suddenly put in an appearance at our bungalow. He sought Mr. Marston's study and told him how Korno Siga had given him the sacred book, and how he had studied it for the months previous, until he had decided to visit the missionary and ask for Christian baptism.

The missionary asked him if he realized how much he must suffer by way of persecution if he became a Christian. "Your tribe have taken the Hindoo religion, and if you become a Christian your people will cast you out, calling you a Christian dog. Your family will forsake you; your property will be confiscated, and you will become a homeless wanderer. Can you endure all this for the sake of a religion of which you only heard six months ago, and which none of your tribe have embraced?"

Habe replied: "I have enjoyed such happiness and such liberty of soul during these months since I believed in Christ, that I can endure all you have mentioned and even more for his sake."

And so he was baptized and went back to his village. The results were just as the missionary had predicted. His brothers took his land from him, his wife and children forsook him, and he was obliged to build him a little hut and live by himself. Often was he spit upon and called a Christian dog, by those who had formerly treated him with deference. Quietly and conscientiously did Habe endeavor to live out the principles which Christ inculcated before his people, and whenever opportunity offered, he earnestly besought them to study Christ's word and life, and see for themselves what this new doctrine could do for them. When the time came for the gathering in of the rice crop every available person in the villages was called into service. The rainy season was fast coming, and the rice must be gathered and stored quickly. The villagers did not ask Habe to help them, feeling that after persecuting him as they had, he would never lend them a helping hand. But unsolicited, he worked day and night for the saving of their crops, though his brothers had defrauded him of all his land. When at length it was all gathered, the people gathered about Habe's hut, and asked him to tell them of his religion. They had never before known a man among them to work day and night for his enemies and persecutors, and they had decided that Habe must have some spirit moving him, of which they were ignorant. Gladly did the good man open to them the beautiful life and doctrines of the divine Christ, and they heard and believed until one after another joined him, and a brotherhood of Christians was organized, and finally the whole village where Habe lived became Christians. They built a church and a school, and Habe became their preacher and teacher. His wife and family came back to him and embraced his faith, and thus his home and all of his surroundings were more comfortable than they had ever been.

Mr. Marston had supplied Habe with American implements of agriculture, so that much larger crops were now raised, and the villages about wished to learn the secret of Habe's successful farming.

One of the *gong buras* (head men) of a Hindoo village begged to use one of the American plows, that he might turn up the soil deeper than the forked stick used by the Hindoos for plows could possibly do. A Hindoo priest seeing him plowing with the Christian plow, commanded him to "put it up at once," telling him that he was "plowing up the sacred religion of the Hindoos with that Christian plow."

Korno Sigo's influence for good among his people was felt all through his tribe. One day when Mr. Marston and myself were travelling with him through the jungle, we came upon an image of a Hindoo god, which a priest had left on the hills, hoping that the people there would become worshippers of idols. Korno Siga threw the image face downward to the ground, and stamping upon it before a large number of his people, said: "Let no one worship this image until it arises and shows its face. This god is more helpless than a babe; who wants to worship such a thing? Our God is eternal and all-powerful, and can save to the uttermost." One night during our journeyings among the hill people we arrived at a late hour in a heathen village where we supposed the people knew nothing of us, nor of the Christian religion. Being exceedingly weary we pitched our little tent, and at once retired to rest. We had scarcely fallen asleep when we were awakened by the voices of singers breaking the stillness of the night air, and as we listened we heard the sweet hymns of our childhood, sacred to us by association with loved parents and relatives in our beloved native land: "Jesus, Lover of my soul," "Rock of Ages cleft for me," and others equally familiar. Wearied and homesick we had laid us down to sleep, and now listening to these familiar words we seemed once more surrounded by our loved absent ones. Mr. Marston went out in search of the singers, and found not one familiar face among them. "Where did you learn these Christian hymns?" he asked. "Korno Siga and Kache taught them to us once when they sojourned a few weeks in our village," was the reply. These hymns became texts for sermons often afterwards among this people.

CHAPTER XV.

HASHISH, OPIUM AND CHRISTIAN BRANDY.

THE Hindoos of Assam are all inveterate smokers. Men, women and children all smoke tobacco and chew the betel nut. It is not an uncommon thing for a toddling infant to leave off nursing and run to its father for a smoke.

Most of the adults also use opium in some form. The hill tribes have never until recent years been opium eaters, nor have the Hindoos known of the use of brandy as a beverage until Christian countries taught them the use of it. Among our people in Assam the common name for all of the intoxicating drinks was *Christian* brandy. The hill tribes make a fermented drink from rice, and are in the habit of drinking it daily as the German does his lager, but they seldom become intoxicated with this drink. The curse of the Hindoo is opium, and it is exceedingly difficult to break one from this terrible habit.

Hashish, the Indian hemp, is called *Bhang* by the Assamese. India is the native country of this plant, and when it is cultivated in northern latitudes it does not produce the resinous exudation that characterizes it in India, which is known by the medical term of *Cannabis Indica.* The large leaves and seed vessels are also used by the common people for the manufacture of this drug. Its effect upon different individuals varies widely. Some are soothed and made serenely happy; others are moved to immoderate and boisterous mirth; while a third class become wrathful and violent and attempt to destroy the lives of others as well as of themselves. Bajan, a Nepaulese servant whom we had in our employ, was of this latter class, though a most valuable employé when not "*Bhanged.*" When in his frantic state from the effects of hashish, he would endeavor to choke himself, and everybody else, seeming to have a mania for catching at necks, and it would require two or three men to control him. The delightful hallucinations produced by this drug give reason to believe that it is the *nepenthe,* or "grief assuager" of the ancients. One of its names in Assam is "causer of the reeling gait," and another "the laughter-mover."

Our word assassin is derived from this word hashish. Hassan ben Sabah founded the eastern branch of assassins. His creed was: "Nothing is true and everything is lawful." He had a fine, well-fortified castle called Alamut, surrounded by walled gardens filled with beautiful flower beds, fruit trees, rippling streams and luxurious halls. Charming maidens and handsome boys were kept in these gardens to entertain visitors. Those whom he considered strong and brave enough to be initiated into the order of assassins, were invited to the banquets of the Grand Master Hoben ben Sabah, and when well intoxicated with hashish they were carried into the beautiful garden and laid upon couches that they might sleep off its effects. On awakening they thought that they were in paradise, and henceforth became most devoted servants of the Grand Master, and willingly undertook all the desperate deeds of violence which he exacted from them. These desperadoes were then called Hashashin, and this word was afterwards corrupted by the Crusaders into assassin, and has continued to this time to be the English term for a cruel, secret murderer. This order of Hashashin was found only a few years ago to have an existence in India, a suit being brought into the English court by a Grand Master who thus sought to recover possession of the records of his order.

The Thugs of India were for a long time the terror of all travellers. These were a sect of assassins who were worshippers of the goddess Kali, the divinity of sensuality and death. She is represented as always thirsting for human blood, and the victims—buffaloes and goats—which are continually sacrificed to her in India are legion. Formerly many human sacrifices were offered to this bloody goddess, but the humanity and Christian principle of the English government has long since forbidden human sacrifices. The Kalika Purana, one of the sacred books of the Hindoos, gives most minute details about the way the Thugs are to conduct their deeds of violence. Each gang had a leader, a guru, or teacher, and learners. Among the latter were stranglers, entrappers and grave-diggers. They assumed the garb of travellers, and they used a handkerchief for strangling their victims. The plunder of this cruel sect was divided into thirds—Kali receiving one-third, the widows and orphans of the sect one-third, and the remaining third to the assassins themselves. We are all familiar with the story of the extermination of the Thugs by the English government. Between 1826 and 1835 nearly two thousand persons in India were condemned as Thugs, and their families were taken under the protection of the government, their children being taught trades and educated to a moral and useful life. Hashish was the drug that these Thugs used, to nerve them up to their deeds of violence. The burglar of America gets along successfully in his vocation of plunder and murder without hashish.

The poppy fields of Bengal are one of the beautiful sights which meet the traveller on his journey through the country. There are two varieties; one with either red or white flowers and black seeds, and the other with pure white flowers and white seeds. The white variety has crimson stripes and lines upon a pure white ground; it is very beautiful and ornamental, and these peculiar traits can be secured by planting only the best seeds from the best flowers. In India the opium poppy is sown in winter, and the soil is highly enriched and abundantly watered. The word opium is derived from the word "opion," meaning poppy juice. In India, incisions with a knife of three or more blades are made in the green capsules; this is done during the hottest part of the day, and the next morning the white juice which has exuded and thickened is scraped off, and put into jars and sent to the opium factories, where it is purified and sent to the market.

The English government still monopolizes the opium trade in India, for though any one may engage in the cultivation of the plant, the opium must all be sold at prices fixed by government; and as India furnishes at least 11,000,000 pounds annually for the market, the revenue realized by the government is enormous. The opium-eaters and smokers are numerous in Assam, a large majority of the Hindoos using it daily in one form or another. To this fact their weak and feeble physical condition is largely owing.

The *hookah* or hubble-bubble is the native apparatus for smoking. This pipe has a long stem which carries the smoke through a cocoanut shell filled with water, and as it is being drawn through it produces a bubbling sound; hence the name hubble-bubble.

The wizened appearance of the Assamese is a painful sight to the European newly arrived in Assam. It is exceedingly difficult to persuade a Hindoo to give up either his betel nut, his tobacco, or his opium, although he knows that the opium at any rate is fast destroying his noblest powers, and rendering him a poor sleeping imbecile. Especially is this true of the older people. And yet the most heroic efforts are made by those who are converted to Christianity to leave off the habit. Some of them even begged that they might be kept in close confinement and suffered to die, rather than be allowed to partake of the accursed drug, which they knew not only ruined their own moral and mental capacities, but also disgraced the pure religion which they had espoused. The young people of Assam are not using it as much as formerly, and our hill people as a rule do not use it. One evening during a religious service I observed Korno Siga dozing in such a manner that I felt quite sure he had been taking opium. I sent for him the next day, and put the question directly to him: "Have you contracted that dreadful habit of smoking opium?" He burst into tears and confessed that he had been using it for six months, and, furthermore, that he had also been partaking of *Christian* brandy.

I was astonished that one who had seemed morally and religiously so strong should have taken on these dreadful habits, and I entreated him as he loved his own soul and cared for the good of his people, that he would at once resolve to "taste not, touch not, handle not," either of these poisons.

At our next meeting of the church-members he made a most penitent confession, and asked that his name be taken from the list of membership, for, said he, "It is not just to the good fruit that the decayed and imperfect should remain in the basket," and ringing his hands and smiting upon his breast, he exclaimed, "Oh, how weak I am! just like a little child who is constantly falling down, and needs some one to help it on its feet. Can I ever be strong and true like the Marston Saheb?"

Mr. Marston refused to have his name stricken from the church list, for, said he, "if Korno Siga is weak he all the more needs the help of the church, and that is what the church is for—to raise the fallen and to strengthen the weak and instruct the ignorant." It was a long time before Korno Siga would trust himself to go into the bazaars or other places where opium was being smoked or whiskey being sold, and he did break himself of these habits.

In order truly to benefit any people we must bear with them in their infirmities, and never despair of them even though they sin against themselves seventy times seven. What a lesson of infinite patience has Christ taught us in his dealings with poor weak humanity! "In all their afflictions he was afflicted," etc., "and he bore them all the days of old." These Assamese converts do really learn to make sacrifices for the good of others. They who know not what real self-denial is may learn a lesson from the following incident, which occurred during the days of famine in Assam. The little body of Christians who had been sorely pressed for food, being obliged to gather the grass seeds and subsist upon them, as there was no rice, had kept up their weekly offerings for carrying the word to the regions beyond during the absence of the missionary from the station. And when the famine abated they brought their money, and putting it into the treasury were about to depart, when they were asked why they had not taken that money and sending to Calcutta bought rice for their hungry families. The reply was, "Teacher, do you think we could *eat* the *Lord's* money?"

CHAPTER XVI.

KORNO SIGA AND THE THIBETAN BUDDHIST.

OUR hero's faith in Christianity was assailed most vigorously by a Buddhist from Thibet, who had come to Assam to sell woollen cloths, shawls and blankets. For the first time, Korno Siga had come in contact with an educated Buddhist, and he found himself quite unable to answer the arguments brought forward to prove that Christianity was only a kind of second edition of Buddhism. He therefore invited the Buddhist to accompany him to Mr. Marston's study, and as he introduced him to Mr. Marston, he frankly admitted that the arguments brought forward by the Thibetan were beyond his ability to answer.

Buddhist. "Our Buddha, Sakya Muni, was born at least four centuries before Christ; he came from heaven; was born of a virgin; was welcomed by angels; received by an aged saint, who was endowed with prophetic vision; was persecuted in the temple; baptized with water, and afterwards baptized with fire. He astonished the most learned doctors by his understanding and his answers. He was led by the spirit into the wilderness, and having there been tempted by the devil and resisted him, he went about preaching and doing wonderful works. He was the friend of publicans and sinners; was transfigured on a mount; descends to hell and ascends to heaven. With the exception of Christ's crucifixion, almost every incident in the life of your Christ is found narrated in the Buddhistic traditions of the life of Sakya Muni Gautama Buddha."

Mr. Marston. "My Buddhist brother, do I understand you to assert that our Christian Scriptures, which we call the New Testament, owe their origin to the legend of Buddha?"

Buddhist. "Yes, that is my assertion, Saheb."

Mr. Marston. "You think that our New Testament writers had in some way become familiar with the Buddhistic legend, but I think I can show you that this could not have been the case. There is no historical record, nor can it be proved that Buddhistic doctrines were at all circulated in Palestine previous to the writing of the Gospel of Jesus Christ. Buddhism, so far as we can learn, was still confined to India, until the reign of Asoka, B. C. 250. It was during the first century of the Christian era that Buddhism reached China. None of the Buddhist authorities make any claim that their missionaries undertook to convert the people on the shores of the Mediterranean. (Dr. Eitel's three lectures on Buddhism.) Moreover, I think you will find that the alleged similarity between your original Buddhistic legend and our Scriptures does not really exist."

Buddhist. "But, Saheb, I have here one of our own legends; read for yourself."

Mr. Marston. "That is one of the more modern legends written after our New Testament was written. I have the most ancient history of Buddha extant, and with your permission I will read to you the sketch of this wonderful man's life. 'Sakya Muni was born in an Aryan village, about one hundred miles north of Benares. His father, Raja Suddhodana, was king of the Sakyas. His mother's name was Maya, and she was forty-five years old when Buddha was born. She died when Buddha was seven days old, and his aunt Prajapatni became his foster-mother. Concerning his childhood and youth the Buddhistic history is silent. When twenty-nine years of age he married his cousin Yasodhara, by whom he had one son, Rahula. At this time, being weighed down by a sense of human misery everywhere visible about him, he determined to renounce home, wife, child, kingdom and all, and give himself to the work of understanding the mystery of sorrow, and removing it if possible. This step is, by the Buddhist authorities, called the "Great Renunciation." He went from one to another of the

Brahmin teachers seeking to learn the way to the cessation of pain, but failing to get relief he gave up all teachers, and took up a life of penance and self-mortification. Then comes that final struggle of Gautama with the spirit of evil, when he discovers the "Four Noble Truths," viz.: 1, The Fact of Sorrow; 2, The Cause of Sorrow; 3, The Destruction of Sorrow; and 4, The Way, the eightfold path that leads to the quieting of pain. From this time Buddha began with missionary zeal to preach the way to others. But the way which he prescribed was not popular with the people, as it involved the adoption of celibacy and the leading of a mendicant life, and thus broke up families, and if reduced to practice would put an end to society. The end of all this was Nirvana, the end of pain, the absence of all desire. Buddha died at the age of eighty, and one of the records says that his death was caused by eating unsuitable food. Many of the humane and philanthropic measures which are attributed to Buddha were really instituted by Asoka, who lived between two and three centuries later.'"

Buddhist. "But, Saheb, you have not yet answered my argument respecting the likeness between Buddhism and Christianity: how do you account for it?"

Mr. Marston. "I think it can be positively shown that the things in Buddhism which Christianity, according to your idea, has borrowed, were on the contrary borrowed from Christianity by the latter Buddhistic legends. For instance, the idea of an infinite, self-existent, omniscient Buddha does not appear in any of the old Buddhistic authorities, but was invented several centuries after the birth of Christ, and in its present full form did not appear until the tenth century of our era, fifteen hundred years after the days of Buddha. Thus do we find by most careful inquiry and research, that the original Manual of Buddha does not so much as teach the existence of a God. On the contrary, it says, 'All being exists from some cause; but that cause is undiscoverable.' Buddhism then is agnosticism, and agnosticism is virtually atheism. The differences between Christianity and Buddhism are wide and radical; Christ was born in poverty; the Buddha in the palace of a king. Christ was born of a virgin; Buddha was the son of the Rajah and Rani of the Sakyas. Christ was never in need of salvation himself, but proclaimed himself the very God. The Buddha is represented as in sore need of salvation, and ignorant how to obtain it, until by long penance and self-sacrifice he found the way to Nirvana, which we can hardly call salvation, since Buddha says, 'If thou keepest thyself silent as a broken gong, thou hast attained to Nirvana.' The Buddha died at a ripe old age; the Christ in his early manhood gives himself to crucifixion that he may save the world. Of what avail are a few seeming agreements between religions which present such wide and radical contrasts? Let me urge upon you, my Thibetan brother, the further investigation of this most interesting of subjects, and come again and let us talk it over."

From this conversation Korno Siga saw how necessary it was that he should thoroughly study the religions of the world, if he would be able to defend his Christian faith successfully with those who sincerely differed from him.

All that could be found relative to the religion of Buddha he now gathered together, and commenced a most careful investigation as to its claims upon the world as a religion sent from God. In this search he most cordially invited the Thibetan Buddhist to join him, and they took for their first investigation the ten commandments as given by Buddha, viz.: 1. Not to deprive any living thing of life. 2. Not to lie. 3. Not to steal. 4. Not to commit adultery. 5. Not to drink what can intoxicate. 6. Not to eat at prohibited seasons. 7. Not to wear wreaths; or use dentifrices or perfumes. 8. Not to sleep on a high or broad bed. 9. To abstain from dancing, music, and stage plays. 10. To abstain from the use of gold or silver.

"As to the first commandment," said the Buddhist, "the Sakya Muni tells us that we break it whenever we kill a louse, bug or tick."

"But," said Korno Siga, "you are breaking that law every time you eat a mango."

"Not so," replied the Buddhist, "for I always eat them in the dark so that I cannot see the worms."

"You well know they are there, however, and you are not a good Buddhist if you thus evade the teachings of your law. Moreover you are destroying life in immense quantities in every drink of water you take, for the missionaries have often shown me myriads of little creatures, called infusoria, in a drop of the river water placed upon the object-holder of a microscope. And they say the little animals are always present in ponds, lakes and rivers."

"But I carry always with me a lota of water from the sacred Brahmapootra, and surely the Hindoo gods keep that free from animal life."

Korno Siga put a drop of the water from the lota under the microscope which stood on the table in the Saheb's study where they were seated, and when the Buddhist saw that it literally swarmed with life, he smote his breast and exclaimed, "Hai, hai, moi pani arn pibo nuarun—Alas, alas, I can never more drink water. Who knows how many of my ancestors I may already have swallowed?"

The doctrine of transmigration of souls is a source of endless worry and concern to Buddhist and Brahmin alike. They fear to kill a snake or a flea, lest their great-grandfather's soul may have taken up its abode in these forms.

How wonderfully different all this, from the liberty of the Christian doctrine and the hope of immortality beyond the grave!

That there are many beautiful moral precepts found in both Buddhist and Brahmin Shasters, no one acquainted with these books will for one moment deny. Indeed is there not something good in every religion and among every people? But when one has lived among a people until he has learned to think in their language, and when he has learned to reason from the Buddhist's and Brahmin's standpoint, and sees things as they really understand them, and not as a beautiful poem like "The Light of Asia" represents them, then indeed, and then only can these ancient religions be justly comprehended. The desire to exalt Buddhism above Christianity seems to me to arise from a desire to escape the heart-searching command of Christ: If any man will do the will he shall know of the doctrine. Did the Thibetan Buddhist become a Christian after the long talks with the missionary and Korno Siga? Oh, no, he went back to his praying wheels which he considered more efficacious than vocal prayer, and to the lamas, hoping that he might sell enough woollen cloths and blankets before his death, so that he might have riches sufficient to hire the lamas when he was about to die to pull the skin from his skull, and make a hole large enough to let out the soul, that he may next become a toad, a snake, or a flea, and thus go on in the transmigrations. Buddha is derived from the Sanscrit word "to know," "to have wisdom," "to understand." The Thibetan Buddhists differ in many respects from those of Burmah, Ceylon and China. In the cold high regions of Thibet, one Buddhist woman may have ten husbands. The praying machine is a little wooden drum covered with leather, and decorated with texts and charms. These are found everywhere among the Thibetan Buddhists; often they are fitted into niches in the walls, and generally arranged in rows of eight or ten. The worshipper has simply to turn the machine with his hand, as inside of it are many prayers written on little scrolls, and each revolution of the wheel counts to the religious credit as many hundred prayers. Some of these praying wheels are small enough to be carried in the hand, while others are of colossal size, and require wind and water to move them. I have somewhere read of one plate in a praying wheel which contained several thousand open dots; and each dot to be filled, when the name of Buddha had been repeated a hundred or a thousand times, with paper, which when burned is supposed to pass into the other world (*i. e.*, his next transmigration) to the credit of the devotee. The Brahmins often name their children after the Hindoo gods, and each time they call the child by name they believe that they are credited with a prayer to that god. The kindness to animals, which is quite characteristic of Brahmins and Buddhists, is largely due to the belief that their friends at death pass into animal forms, and in hurting or killing one of these animals they might be destroying the habitations of grandfathers and uncles. A company of these people when about to seat themselves on their mats, will brush away carefully every vestige of dust from them, lest perchance they might sit upon ants and destroy their aunts.

In pure Buddhism, no god is mentioned, and this religion has never yet advanced a nation higher than China or Siam. One has very aptly said of it: "The highest conception of Buddhism is to be unselfish for the selfish end of attaining a solitary Nirvana in which one shall desire neither existence nor non-existence." And yet who shall say that this religion has not, like all those preceding Christ's advent to the earth, been a looking forward to, and in some measure a preparation for, the highest and best in the revelation of the immaculate and divine Son of God, the world's Redeemer?

Prof. Max Muller, in his "Science of Religion," says: "We have ignored or wilfully narrowed the sundry times and divers manners in which God spoke in times past unto our fathers, the prophets. If we believe there is a God, and that he created heaven and earth, and that he ruleth the world by his overseeing providence, we cannot believe that millions of human beings, all created like ourselves in the image of God, were in their time of ignorance abandoned by God; so that their religion was a farce and their whole life a mockery. An honest and impartial study of the religions of the world will teach us that it was not so; that there is no religion which does not contain some grains of truth. It will teach us to see in the study of the ancient religions more clearly than anywhere else, the divine education of the human race."

This all being pre-eminently true, are we not, nevertheless, in danger of overestimating Buddhism in this our day? Let me quote here a note of warning from Robert Burdette: "Who is Buddha? Did you ever notice, my son, that the man who tells you he cannot believe in the Bible is usually able to believe in almost anything else? You will find men who will turn with horror and utter disbelief of the Bible, and joyfully embrace the teachings of Buddha. It is quite the thing just now for a civilized, enlightened man, brought up in a Christian country and an age of wisdom, to be a Buddhist. And if you ask six men who profess Buddhism, who Buddha was, one of them will tell you he was an Egyptian soothsayer who lived two hundred years before Moses. Another will tell you that he brought letters from Phœnicia and introduced them into Greece; a third will tell you that she was a beautiful woman of Farther India, bound by her vows to perpetual chastity; a fourth will, with a little hesitation, say he was a Brahmin of the ninth degree, a holy disciple of Confucius; and of the other two, one will frankly admit that he does not know, and the other will say, with some indecision, that he was either a Dervish of the Nile (whatever that is), or a Felo de se, he can't be positive which. Before you propose to know more than anybody and everybody else, my son, be very certain that you are abreast of at least two-thirds of your fellow-men. I don't want to suppress any inclination you may have towards genuine free thought and careful honest investigation. I only want you to avoid the great fault of atheism in this day and generation. I don't want you to try and build a six-story house on a one-story foundation. Before you criticise, condemn and finally revise the work of creation, be pretty confident that you know something about it as it is, and don't, let me implore you, don't turn this world upside down and sit on it and flatten it entirely out, until you have made or secured another one for the rest of us to live in while you demolish the old one."

CHAPTER XVII.

TEA CULTIVATION, AND OTHER INDUSTRIES OF ASSAM.

SCATTERED throughout the province of Assam are many tea gardens, superintended almost entirely by Europeans from England and Scotland. But few Yankees have as yet entered that line of work. The plant is indigenous to the country, and before the advent of Europeans the natives were in the habit of frying the green leaves in mustard oil and eating them as greens. The great "boom" in tea cultivation took place while I was living in Assam, and though there followed a reaction from that unhealthy period of tea excitement, the enterprise has been a success, and the tea annually sent home from Assam by the planters is an excellent article, very favorably known in commerce and bringing a good price. One of the great difficulties which the tea planter has to contend with is the necessity of importing coolies from Calcutta to work the tea gardens. This is very expensive, and the coolies are often dissatisfied and sickly, and give the poor planter any amount of *dukh*, trouble. It seems to us that the

English government has not been in sympathy with the tea planters, as would be naturally supposed it would. On the contrary, the sums required for the lease of lands, which one would think the government would only be too glad to have cultivated without receiving tax money, are enormously high and exacting, and we wonder that the planters are able to realize any gain after their heavy expenses.

The planters are in many ways a blessing to Assam as well as to the tea-drinking world. Their hardships and privations are many, and being obliged to live on their gardens they have but little European society, and live very lonely lives. In the early days of the tea cultivation a planter might sicken and die without an European knowing of his fate. One planter, but twenty miles from us, was attacked with cholera, died and remained in his bed two weeks before his European friends knew aught of it. I verily believe that the missionaries have a much easier life in every way than the tea planters of Assam. And the planters have it in their power to do real missionary work among their employés, if they are so inclined; and they do occasionally show themselves both philanthropic and truly Christian in their efforts to benefit the miserable coolies who work for them. The planters have been much censured for not observing the Sabbath on their gardens more generally. Their plea is that they must lose two days' work if they keep the Sabbath, as the leaves picked on Saturday cannot wait until Monday to be dried. Still when there comes to be an earnest desire to observe the Sabbath, there will be some way found out of this difficulty. It is no small matter to clear the land of forest trees, thoroughly break up the soil, and get ready for the tea planting. The money required is considerable, and the work quite similar to clearing a farm in New England.

After the young plants are set out, the weeds must be carefully cleared away, the soil frequently stirred to allow the plants to get all possible nourishment from mother earth, and even then it takes three years to get a plantation in condition to produce tea. The tea plant, if left to grow without pruning, will become a tall tree, but the planters find that the yield of leaves is better when they are kept to about five feet in height. The plant is much like the English myrtle bush, and has white blossoms which resemble small dog-roses. Teas are black or green, according to the age of the leaf and the manner in which it is manipulated. If a plant is sickly, the leaves are not picked from it. Indeed, all the leaves are not taken at one time from a plant. It is customary to make nursery beds every year so that there may be a constant succession of new plants. The slopes of the hills are the sites usually chosen for the gardens in Assam. The soil here is free from stagnant moisture. Most beautiful to my eyes were these gardens in appearance as I travelled through the hills. I have spent hours in their study and admiration, and often thought that I would like to be engaged in this work, and make my plantation a wholesale missionary centre, having a school, a church and a hospital conducted on a thrifty Yankee plan. The finest teas are made from the half-open buds, which are always the first gathering, the younger the leaves the more delicate their flavor. The finest teas of Assam are but rarely seen in America. The maximum yield of the plants is in their eighth or tenth year. There are five or six gatherings in the course of a year, and each time the leaves are coarser than the preceding gathering. The gathering can only be done in clear weather, and the best teas are from leaves gathered in the afternoon, when they are thoroughly dry and warm. The hill tribe women are the best pickers in Assam, and if I remember correctly, gather on an average forty pounds a day. It takes four pounds of leaves to make one of tea, and I believe the usual estimate is that ten thousand pounds of tea can annually be marketed from one hundred thousand plants. Green tea is made from leaves which have been roasted immediately after they are gathered, and are then rolled and dried. Black teas are from leaves which have been exposed to sun and air for half a day or more for drying, and, if the weather is damp, artificial heat is used. The roasting is done over a sort of stove which is heated by charcoal, and a man manipulates the leaves constantly, so that none may stick to the pan and burn. The rolling has formerly been done by the hands (or feet) of the natives, placing as much tea as the hands will cover on a mat. The motion is such that it gives each leaf a twist on itself as one rolls them from right to left. Then there is a second roasting and a second rolling. Shallow pans are used for roasting black tea, but the green tea requires deep pans. The teas are put into a long basket after the final roasting, and submitted to the heat over a charcoal fire for several minutes, when they are poured out and receive another rolling. Then the leaves are sifted, and winnowed, and fried once more to remove every vestige of moisture, and finally packed in chests and sent away to the market.

The native industries are confined almost altogether to the cultivation of rice, tobacco, sugarcane, and mustard oil. Something has been done by them also in the way of gathering the caoutchouc which exudes from the rubber trees, and sending it to Calcutta to market. Our hill people did considerable of that work and realized fine remuneration. The caoutchouc as it first exudes from the incisions made in the trees, is of a white color, and as they wind it into balls it takes on a brownish red appearance as it is exposed to the air.

The silk-worm thrives in Assam, and all of the better clothes of the Assamese of the plains are made by the women, who cultivate the plants on which to feed the silk-worms, and also spin and weave the thread into clothes for their families.

Cotton clothing is their more common apparel. Their embroidered borders and fringes are quite beautiful, and a native high-caste woman in full dress presents a very graceful and pretty sight.

The implements for cultivating are of a rude kind, and the priests forbid them to adopt modern improved machinery of all kinds. The plows merely scratch the surface of the soil. The religious prejudices of the people forbid them to use the manure of cows for enriching the soil; the cow being a sacred animal, the manure is largely devoted to religious purposes, the Fakirs (religious mendicants) covering their heads and bodies with it, to render themselves acceptable to the gods. A well-regulated Assamese hut must be lipped, plastered over, with the cows' manure every morning, in order to keep it pure and acceptable to the Hindoo deities.

Rice is the staple grain, and two crops are

raised annually, viz.: the dry and the wet season crop. Millet, peas and many varieties of pulse and grain are also raised. The manner of expressing the oil from the mustard seed is primitive among the villagers. I have seen a whole family make weights of themselves for six or seven consecutive days, as they have the mustard seeds under a huge log, and they all seat themselves upon it. The much enjoyed *hookah* keeps up its hubble-bubble constantly, as it is passed from one member to another of this happy family.

I have ventured at times to suggest that a weight of less importance than human flesh might be employed. But my suggestion has usually been answered by the head of the family, "Etu dostur amar," "This is our custom," which is with him considered an unanswerable argument. How different this from American ways!

You ask if it would pay a young man to go from America to engage in business in Assam. Yes, if he can get a position as superintendent of a tea garden, or take charge of an ice manufacturing establishment, or if he has a little capital ahead so that he could engage in the lumber or coal business. There are vast resources of this kind awaiting Yankee energy and perseverance; but it does not answer for us to depend upon the natives to any extent in earning one's livelihood. The time will come, however, is indeed near at hand, when the

English government will open up all the province of Assam to railroad and telegraphic communication, and this will work wonders in the development of all kinds of business advantages.

At present the only means of reaching the mineral products of the hills, the coal, iron, gold-dust, and petroleum, is by long and dangerous journeys through dense jungles infested with beasts of prey and reeking with malaria. The steamers which ply the large rivers do not approach near enough to many of these storehouses of nature, for men to avail themselves of this means of transport. But the day of railroads draws on apace, and we will await with patience its advent.

CHAPTER XVIII.

A DAY OF DARKNESS.

I CANNOT re-write the details of this darkest of all days, and hence copy from letters written during that period to my home circle in America.

"For five days I have tried in vain to tell you the sad, sad news of my bereavement. It came upon me so suddenly and I was so weak that I could only lie still and cry to God. I seemed all alone and in the dark, till the loving Saviour came and spake such sweet comforting words, that I opened my eyes and found that there was yet light for me in heaven, even though my earthly light had gone out. And since that hour I have gradually come back again to life. Henry has gone to meet the Saviour he loved and served so faithfully here. On Tuesday morning he was awakened from a quiet rest and sleep, with symptoms of cholera, which disease has raged fearfully in our district during the past month. Our little Henry being only three weeks old, I was not allowed to know that my dear husband was ill until about an hour after he was attacked. Remedies for cholera were given at once and the symptoms abated for a while, but only to set in with renewed violence, when cholera in its worst form was unmistakably claiming him for its victim. The English doctor, his wife, and our deputy commissioner all came and most kindly assisted in every way possible, and in a few hours the dreadful pains and cramps had ceased and he lay quietly resting, only being disturbed that we might administer stimulants and nourishment.

"He seemed so free from pain, that I said to him: 'I will go and look after our babe, for he is very hungry.' He drew me down and kissed me, and held my hand for some time.

"I asked: 'Have you any pain?'

"'None at all,' was the reply.

"'Are you at peace in your mind?'

"He looked up, and with a beaming face replied, 'Perfect peace.'

"I had left him but a moment when the deputy commissioner came to me to say that he wished I would come and give Henry his medicine, as he would not take it from his hand. I went at once, and as soon as I looked into my dear husband's face, I knew that the arrow of death had pierced his heart, and that the kind-hearted commissioner had not the courage to tell me all the truth. Henry did not recognize me, and in less than five minutes he had breathed his last. He sank away as calmly and as sweetly as a little child goes to sleep in its mother's arms. He leaned his head on Jesus' breast, and breathed his life out sweetly there.

"Soon after he was attacked in the morning he had noticed my anxious look, and said, 'Don't feel anxious, my dear; I have committed you and our sweet babes to God. He will take better care of you than I can.'

"Henry has not been well for several weeks. His anxiety for me, his constant ministrations night and day to the poor natives, the dead and the dying demanding his care, and the whole burden of church, school, and family being upon him, were too much for him. He has seemed very near to the heavenly world for many months. His talk of heaven and his ardent longing to be absent from the body and present with his Lord, has told me only too plainly that my angel guide was not long to be with me. Oh, that I may be as ripe for the heavenly garners as he!

"I beseech you to break the sad tidings gently to his aged father. Tell him that the angel of death came to me on Tuesday morning, and asked me for his only son, and that I fell before him and besought him if one must go that I might be that one, and that Henry, so capable, so noble and so useful, might be spared. But the messenger of death sadly shook his head. And then one after another I offered him my precious children. 'No,' he said, 'the Master calls for this chosen one; he is ripe for heaven.' He died at four in the afternoon and was buried at the same hour the day following; the beautiful burial-service of the English church being read by our commissioner.

"And so I am alone in a heathen land, with three little ones clinging helplessly to me. Alone, and yet not alone, for the Saviour is with me by day and night and has taken from me the bitterness of death. He will be a father to my children and will be the widow's God. I have written to two of my missionary associates, a hundred miles distant from me, asking them to come to our station, should the plague take me away, and care for the children until they go to America. Were it not for these little ones, I should only be too glad to go and join my beloved on the other side of the river. But for their sakes, I am willing to live and wait patiently the time when God shall pronounce my life-work done and gather us an unbroken family in heaven.

"It will be a source of comfort to all at home, to know that all that human love could do was done for Henry. You know how every one loved him who knew him, and that was quite as true of him here as at home. The beautiful flowers of Assam of which he was so fond were all about the precious corpse and little Ruth says: 'Papa is sleeping in a nice box.'

"Paul has grieved himself ill for his father. After trying in vain to comfort him I said: 'Paul, you know your father has gone to a brighter and happier place to live, and we must not grieve for him, but live so that we may go to live with him.'

"He replied: 'Mamma, that is just what I feel so sad about. I am afraid papa has not gone to the happy land.'

"'Why, Paul, how can you have such a fear?'

"'Well, papa told me himself that when good people die the thinking part goes to heaven and that which cannot think is buried in the ground. And I looked so closely when they fastened the lid of the casket, and his forehead—papa said that was the thinking part—was still there, and oh, they have buried dear papa's soul.'

"I tried to explain to him that the soul was invisible, and only lived in the body just as we lived in our house, but did not form a part of the house, and the dear little thoughtful boy seemed comforted and has since been quite cheerful.

"Our little band of native Christians are inconsolable and the young men of the Normal School mourn as for an own parent. The native merchants and the people from all the villages far and near have come to express their sympathy and to mourn with me, saying, 'This man was one of the best friends our country ever had.' All have rallied about me and endeavored to comfort me, but how can I be comforted when my dearest earthly friend no more walks with me the path of life?

"I was deeply touched the night after Henry's burial, to see fifteen of our native Christian women come with their mats and their babies and take their places for the night on my verandah, that I might not feel lonely through the long, sleepless hours until the daybreak.

"God has given to Henry some precious fruit in this far-off vineyard, and were it not that my first duty is to my fatherless children, I should have no greater joy than to remain here and carry on his work for these people.

"They have laid him to rest in the unconsecrated part of the cemetery of the Episcopal church; not being a member of the Church of England it was not thought proper that he, a dissenter, should lie in the consecrated ground. There is a line of earth cast up between that which the bishop has consecrated and the other portion. When I ventured to express my regrets to our good deputy commissioner that Henry should lie in unconsecrated ground while the many godless English officers were in the more favored portion, he kindly remarked that 'all the consecration those poor fellows ever had was in their present surroundings, and that Mr. Marston did not need consecrated ground for he was consecration itself!'"

That you may know in what esteem my dear husband was held, I copy here a few of the many testimonials which came to me during those dark days. The dear old Secretary of our Missionary Society, who once told me to await the openings of Providence and who has long ago gone home to heaven, wrote thus:

"The announcement of the death of Mr. Marston is exceedingly painful to us all. We prized him highly for his personal qualities and for his work wrought for the hill tribes of Assam. A manly man was he and a fully developed Christian. In missionary character he stood pre-eminent; few equalled and none, so far as my range of vision extends, surpassed him. He had breadth, tact, facility of movement, persistence and genuine force. I think he possessed an uncommon power to lay hold of men and mould their character. His crowning excellence was his Christian spirit, running through all, giving tone to all and never forsaking him. His devotion was whole hearted, exclusive, a fire that burned to the last moment of his life. His letters had an originality and freshness that always charmed me. He could not write a common-place. Such an eyesight and heart-sight of religion; such a profound view of sin and salvation; such a knowledge of his own heart, its needs and its supplies; so clear and comprehensive ideas of the work before him, and such a grasp on the resources in the gospel; all these came to me as a refreshing solace."

MEMORIAL.

"With morning's earliest beam,
In a far Orient land,
A dream, or more than dream,
Fell on a sleeping band.
'Twas shadow, yet 'twas light,
Like morn's mysterious strife;
'Twas day, and yet 'twas night,
'Twas death, and yet 'twas life.

"A man of God, and she
Who wrought life's psalm with him,
And tender offspring three—
Five bars for their sweet hymn!
For days among life's strings
An unseen hand had felt,
And there were sounds of wings,
Whene'er in prayer he knelt.

"His last words, 'perfect peace,'
Those heavenly beaming eyes,
Proclaim a soul's release,
That ne'er in dying dies!
Raise not a wailing note
For him who now is free
A banner well might float
With shout of victory.

"He fought the Christian's fight
And wears the victor's crown,

And on a throne of light
  Is with his Lord set down.
Not for himself alone
  Truth's banner he unfurled,
The conflict was his own,
  His victory for the world.

"But who are those that stand—
  Those stalwart men in tears?
Ah, 'tis his much loved band
  Of swarthy mountaineers:
He won them for his Lord,
  And tamed each savage breast
By Christ's all conquering word,
  And led them to his rest.
Yea, weep, oh mountain men,
  Around that marble brow:
Ah, who o'er hill and glen
  Shall light your watch-fires now?"

IN MEMORIAM

OF

HENRY C. MARSTON.

"Let the hills bow in grief for the minstrel departed,
  Whose viol and voice could the savages tame;
The wildest of the tribes may lament broken-hearted,
  The friend of Assam they can never more claim.
Yet joy to those hill men whose spirits he gladdened;
  His feet on the mountains had beauty to them;
Though his flight for a season their hearts may have saddened
  In his 'crown of rejoicing' will each be a gem.

"He could not grow weary of work for the Master,
While the heathen around him were shrouded in gloom,
And the plague with its terrors was pleading the faster
For aid to the dying and hope in the tomb.
He could not grow weary, for love, the evangel,
Refreshing his zeal, it could never abate;
And death could not conquer, but came like an angel,
To post him to heaven and open the gate."

On his tombstone are inscribed the following words:

"If life be not in length of days,
In silver locks or furrowed brow,
But living to a Saviour's praise—
How few have lived so long as thou!"

CHAPTER XIX.

LIGHT IN THE DARKNESS.

"It is not dark, that's dark alone
For this our little earthly while;
It is not bright, whose smiling sun
Illumes the day it shines upon
With else than an immortal smile.

"We know not till the middle day,
What tokens best befit the dawn;
The clouds that weep our morn away
Fit, oft, for heaven's serenest ray,
When the full strength of life comes on.

"Oh, say not that the life is blest,
That brightens most our earthly years;
Deem not that life is sorely pressed,
That wrings not from a changeless breast
An immortality of tears!"

SIX months after Henry's death I wrote this letter home. I had stayed on with the "much-loved mountaineers." Indeed, I could not find it in my heart to leave them:

"God has in tender mercy remembered his precious promises to the widow and the fatherless. This season of thick darkness has revealed to me worlds of light I never saw before. Still, at times the sense of loss and loneliness is almost overwhelming, almost too heavy to be borne, exiled as I am from the loved ones of my native land.

"I regret that I have been unable to write to you oftener. But my hands have been very full of work, for the whole care of the mission has been upon me. I have assisted the native preachers in planning and arranging their sermons, have had the charge of the Bible scholars on Sunday and twelve week-day schools, besides caring for the sick and suffering among us.

"I am happy to tell you that I and the children have been perfectly well, and I have had a most excellent *ayah* to take care of them.

"Forty young men are now holding scholarships in our Hill Tribe Normal School and are receiving each 52 rupees ($25) per annum. From this sum they clothe and feed themselves and buy their school-books and stationery. They cannot live luxuriously on this sum, and they economize closely on food and clothes that they may have money to buy books. They are wonderfully eager to learn, and Henry seems to have imparted his own ardent love for knowledge into every one of these young men. In the midst of all their poverty they always manage to have a few pice for those who have never heard of Christ our Lord.

"The government inspector of schools made a

careful examination of the standing of these pupils last week, and thus reports his opinion of it: 'I visited the Hill Tribe Normal School on Monday. You are aware that this was my second visit to the school this year. As before, I was very much pleased with the school: the numbers had increased considerably since my previous visit, and there was evidently great interest taken by the lads in their work. I have formed a good opinion of the teacher's attainments and of his power of teaching. Allow me to suggest that more attention be given by the pupils to dictation and geography. Permit me to assure you that as long as I am at the head of the educational department of this province, any assistance you may need shall be afforded by myself and my subordinates.'

"I hear on every hand good reports from the young men who are teaching and preaching on the hills around about our mission station, and one after another is being gathered into the fold of the Good Shepherd. All the young men of the Normal School are now professing Christians. When they saw their beloved missionary teacher die, they said: 'A religion that can make a man live as he lived, and die as he died, is the religion for us.' And six of these young men have taken upon them the work of preaching the gospel that they may in some measure fill the wide gap left here by

Henry's death. And Habe and Korno Siga seem to have been consecrated anew.

"As for my own plans for the future, I can only say to you, that so long as God gives health to me and to my children, I do not see how I can leave this my chosen work, until I must do so in order to attend to the education of my children. At least my path of duty is plainly set before my eyes to remain until some one shall come to take up the work here; and I am sure I am happier in this work, so dear to my beloved one, and the work to which my own heart has been solemnly pledged even from my childhood's days. So please say to all who are interested in these hill tribe people, that I hope they will not withhold their hearts from praying nor their hands from giving, because the voice of Mr. Marston is silent. Remembering the sore bereavement which has come upon this mission, let more earnest and unceasing prayers be offered for its prosperity, that God will adopt all these orphaned ones into his own family, and get to himself a great name among his people."

I trust I may not be regarded as egotistical if I quote here the testimony of the secretary of our Missionary Society in regard to my work at this period: "Mrs. Marston was at first completely overwhelmed by the death of her husband, but, rising from her great sorrow, she grasped with a steady hand the helm of the mission, and she has wisely and bravely held it ever since. This work with a woman at its head is at once unique and beautiful in every respect."

"I said once, 'Dark and cold,
Ah, cold and dark, the grave to which we tend,
Where lover parts from lover, friend from friend,
And life's brief tale is told,
With its pathetic ending, "Dust to dust."'

"Now, with a new-born faith and loving trust,
I say, 'The grave is blest:'
Oh, call it dark no more, since he is laid
In its still depths, whose life a sunshine made,
In good deeds manifest,
To cheer the gloom of sorrow and despair,
And pour its bright beams round him everywhere.

His blameless life from mean ambitions free,
What loved the right it dared to do and be,
Lessons sublime did give
Of a true nobleness."

CHAPTER XX.

WOMAN'S WORK FOR WOMAN.

IN the spring of 1870 there came to my home in Assam one of those sweet angels of mercy sent out by the Woman's Missionary Societies of America. Miss Margaret Brown was the daughter of a most honored missionary, and she came to us filled with a woman's tender pity for the secluded, degraded women of India.

She was bright and intelligent, highly educated and truly consecrated to her work. Most heartily she entered into all earnest plans for reaching the high-caste women in the Zenanas, and she had breadth and tact sufficient to make an effectual entrance there. These women are graceful and attractive in appearance and exceedingly fond of everything pretty and attractive, and Margaret took advantage of this trait in offering to teach them all kinds of beautiful needle-work and fancy articles. And as she went from house to house among them, she always carried her Bible and hymn-book, and faithfully taught these ignorant ones the way of eternal life.

Her presence in our girls' schools was a benediction, and her pure unaffected love of all good things was to these poor girls an inspiration and an example. Daily did I thank God that there was such a society of women, to send out such valuable helpers to those who were already overburdened with an accumulation of work. How much my children loved this beautiful woman, who was to them both teacher and companion!

I think our people in America can hardly realize what a good work there is to be done among the women and girls of India by educated, Christian ladies. Fully to realize the importance and magnitude of this work one must live in India, and know the social status of East Indian life. I could not believe, until I entered the high-caste home and saw how the women were treated, that human beings brought up in the nineteenth century could think it right to treat women so cruelly. The Brahmin Shasters are largely to blame for this state of things; there is nothing so unreasonable and stubborn as a false religion, and a corrupt priesthood can give almost any meaning to a command which in itself may be harmless. For instance, in the ancient books of Vedaism and Brahminism there is no command for the burning of widows, but the text says, "When a man dies let his widow or widows put on the dun-colored garment peculiar to the widow; let her also put off all her jewels, and ascend up into her house and consecrate herself to the memory of her husband." But a corrupt priesthood have changed the word *house*, which in the Sanscrit language is very similar to the word *fire*, and have made the command that she shall ascend up into the fire, *i. e.*, offer herself upon the funeral pile. The priests used to stand by and receive the jewels as these poor women ascended the pile; and when the English government forever put a stop to this most cruel religious rite, the priests wept and wailed, for the hope of their gain in filthy lucre was gone. Women in India are punished by their husbands, by divers beatings and by the rubbing of red pepper in their eyes. I have often had my righteous soul vexed within me by the cool indifference with which the men would regard the agonizing screams of their wives under such torture.

If a Hindoo woman suffers much in giving birth to her child, her husband and all of her family take that as a positive evidence that she has not been a virtuous woman, and with cruel blows they will stand over her and command her to confess who her guilty paramour is. More than once have I known a woman under such circumstances to confess to a sin of which she has never been guilty. No gentleman physician is ever allowed to see these high-caste women in their times of sickness and suffering. Hence the great need of lady physicians who may minister to these much abused but lovable women. That there should be such a physician at every mission station in India is a most needed arrangement, and Lady Dufferin, realizing the great need of Hindoo women, has nobly organized an association in which the Hindoo gentlemen of wealth are now co-operating by contributing generously to its support. Such measures as these will work great good in India, and will call forth the profound gratitude, to a Christian nation, of all Hindoo women.

One night as I was encamped in a Hindoo village, I heard at midnight the wailing of a woman, and taking one of the Christian men with me I set out to ascertain the cause of her sorrow. I found one of the low-caste Hindoo women seated on the ground with a dead baby clasped to her breast, while she rocked herself to and fro. These were the words of her lamentation: "Oh, Ram, Krishna, Shiva and all Hindoo gods, can you not tell me where my child is gone? It smiles no more upon me; when I call it, it answers me not again. Whither has its spirit fled? Into what form of beast or reptile has its spirit entered? Is there no power, good or evil, that can tell me where to search now for my child? Has it entered into a toad or a snake?" With this last question she shuddered with fear and beat upon her breast and tore her hair in agony of despair. I sat down beside her and told her of the Christian woman's hope: that when our little ones die, we think of them as forever happy, as being in a lovely home where a Father more tender and loving than any mother on earth can be, provides for their every want: where they shall hunger no more, neither thirst any more, and where the intense heat of the sun shall never more trouble them. I told her too of the Christian woman's faith that she shall meet her child, who is called dead, in that beautiful country.

"How can that be?" she asked with a wondering look in her dark eyes. "Our Hindoo religion teaches that women have no souls until they are honored by transmigration with a man's body. How, then, can a woman enter by death into such a beautiful spirit-land?"

I tried to tell her of what Christ's religion had done for woman—how Christ had called her, daughter, and given her positive assurance that she had a place in the paradise of the good where they neither marry nor are given in marriage, but are as the angels.

"How long has it been since the women of your country knew of such a religion?"

"More than eighteen hundred years have passed since Christ was made manifest in the flesh," I replied, "and our women have heard the story from their earliest infancy."

"What have they been doing this long time that they have not sent teachers before to tell us poor Hindoo women of such a blessed religion—a religion that allows mothers to hope to see their dead babies again, and does not send their spirits into snakes and horrid beasts?"

How glad I was to tell her that the women of America and England were at last earnestly engaged in sending teachers everywhere to women who had not heard of this better way.

Miss Brown and I spent happy, useful years together, until the time when I was compelled to take my children from a climate where they no longer could thrive, and place them where they could have the bracing air of a temperate zone, and the educational advantages of a civilized and Christian country. Other workers, noble, earnest men and women, came to take Mr. Marston's and my place, and I bade a tearful farewell to that much loved band of native Christians and "swarthy mountaineers."

Our gentle Margaret Brown stayed on at her post until the "cholera god" came and claimed her too as its victim; and a friend of hers thus beautifully writes of her death:

> "God's angels keep
> His watch o'er those who wake and sleep:
> E'en death, through his providing care,
> Will plant the seed whose fruitage fair
> Of ransomed souls in years to come
> Shall swell the reaper's 'Harvest Home.'

"Yet land bereaved, beloved, for thee
Thy children's tears fall silently.
The sickle dropped, the grain unbound
Stands whitening all the fertile ground,
While scattered laborers strong in faith
Toil on through sufferings unto death.

"Oh, shall the anguish and the tears,
The martyr lives of other years,
Whose agony of soul was given
To lift thy sons from earth to heaven,
Bring forth their future fruit in naught
But tender memory, reverent thought?

"No, the dear ashes scattered wide
By Orient and by Western tide,
Cry, 'Speed the torch from hand to hand,
Till hut and fane illumined stand:
Till warrior, priest and devotee
In one glad worship bend the knee.'

"And let the sound of Sabbath bell
Over thy mountain barriers swell,
Till eastward meet the westward wave,
And in far isle and desert cave
That faith be held, that praise be sung,
Which knows no bound of clime or tongue."

CHAPTER XXI.

HOMEWARD BOUND.

As the years had passed, my heart had become more and more bound up in my work for the people of Assam.

Their weakness and frail moral composition had all the more awakened my lively sympathy and tender affection; even as a mother often finds her heart going out most to the sickly or wayward child. But I loved my own flesh and blood better than all else of an earthly nature, and I knew that I had no right to sacrifice my children's highest interests for the sake of helping the Assamese. Neither Mr. Marston nor Christ would ask or desire me to do that. For two hot seasons Paul had suffered greatly from a disease which seemed impossible to cure, and I feared it might become chronic if I did not get him away from Assam before a third hot season came on. European children thrive well in Assam until they come to be ten or twelve years of age.

When our dear people of Assam learned that we were about to leave them, they gathered for a farewell meeting. They came from the hills and plains, and stayed about the mission compound for days. They wrote poems and farewell letters, and offered resolutions of regret. I have these poems and letters yet, and shall always keep them as legacies of affection from a people I worked for. Some of these are in the hill people's language, some in Assamese and a few in English. One of the English letters from a young Brahmin whom I had instructed for a time in English, commences thus: "Most venerable Madam: One of your ancient pupils, Moses, whom you so graciously taught the English language, writes to tell you how sorry he is that you are to leave our Assam country."

For the word *venerable* he meant *respected*, and for *ancient* pupil he meant *former* pupil.

One mountain chief brought his son and wished to give him to me that I might have him educated in a Christian country, saying that he himself was too old to change his religion, but he wanted Sarlok to be just such a man as Mr. Marston was. The dear native converts and the pupils of my school wept as though their hearts would break, and Korno Siga, as spokesman for all the rest, said: "We shall miss you and mourn for you, and every cold season we shall go to the brow of our highest hill and look far off on the plains to see if you are returning to us. We shall never lie down to sleep at night or arise from our beds in the morning without thinking of you and your precious children, and offering a prayer for your happiness and safe return to us. We shall watch, as the weeks pass away, for your footsteps on the mountains. The Father above took the Marston Saheb to live with himself; surely he will not think best to bereave us forever of the presence of Mem Saheb and the babes."

Another of our native people addressed me in the following parting words: "Beloved teacher: From the land of the setting sun did your husband and yourself come to teach us of the divine Christ. After eight years of earnest work in our behalf the much beloved Saheb, Mr. Marston, went to heaven. His grave shall be tenderly watched and cared for during your absence, and month after month shall we gaze far down the Brahmapootra river to see if you are returning to us. It was a sore trial for us to lose our father, and now our mother goes from us. May your children grow a foot a day so that you may soon leave them in America and return to your sorrowing and more needy children of Assam."

At length the parting words were all said, and as far as we could discern the figures of our friends, they waved their adieus to us as they watched our boat from the banks of the river. None but a missionary can understand the deep affection which binds the converts made from heathenism to their Christian teachers. And the missionary grieves over the fall of one of these little ones almost as deeply as over his own flesh and blood.

We took passage on a steamer to Golunda. Here the children for the first time saw a locomotive, and little Henry was much frightened at it. Clinging to my hand he asked if that was an Assamese devil.

We remained in Calcutta two weeks and enjoyed sight-seeing in the City of Palaces, and spent several evenings in the Eden gardens admiring the beautiful variety of tropical plants and the ornamental architecture of the beautiful Burmese pagoda, which was brought from Prome and reconstructed in the Eden gardens in 1856.

The Post-office on the west side of Delhousie square is a magnificent building, and the Government House is of very imposing appearance. Commodious galleries connect the four wings. This is the residence of the Governor-General, and affords ample accommodation for public entertainment, levees and all official business. Every one who has visited Calcutta has doubtless noticed the Adjutant birds standing for hours on the top of this building. The Ghauts, the Musjeeds, and the monuments of Calcutta aid very materially in making it a city of beautiful appearance. The bishop's palace and the imposing cathedral of St.

Paul are also fine buildings. Here we heard the grand organ, which cost about eight thousand dollars, and looked upon the colossal statue of Bishop Heber, which occupies a place in the northern transept. As we enter under the organ, the choir in its whole dimensions, with the window by Benjamin West, representing the Crucifixion, bursts upon our view.

After attending service at the cathedral, our Paul expressed himself thus emphatically: "I don't like that kind of church service; it is six times and five times, and five times and six times, and I can't keep run of it." He was confused by the frequent kneeling and arising, and this was his manner of expressing his dislike of such a service. As for myself, I enjoyed it most thoroughly.

The shipping of Calcutta presents a very fine appearance. During a severe cyclone while I was in Assam sixty-five large vessels were washed ashore, and great destruction of property was the result. The name Calcutta is written Kali Ghautta in the Hindoostani language, and means the landing place of the goddess Kali, the wife of Shiva, the god of destruction. Her temple formerly stood on the river bank. Fort William is the largest fort in India, and will accommodate fifteen thousand soldiers, and cost about $10,000,000. There are over six hundred cannon kept here.

The dungeon of Fort William, called the Black Hole of Calcutta, where one hundred and twenty-three brave British soldiers were suffocated in 1756 by Surajah Dowlah, the Indian ruler of Bengal, is a place familiar to history, and all philanthropic hearts throb with sympathy as they recall the days of the birth-throes of the British empire in India.

Below Calcutta, on the right bank as we descend the Hoogly, is Garden Reech, one of the beautiful suburbs, with its elegant gardens and handsome European residences; while on the left bank are the famous Botanical Gardens, with the celebrated banyan tree of immense size, whose ever increasing branches spread themselves, taking fresh root.

We took passage in one of the fine steamers of the Peninsula and Oriental line via the Suez Canal to Southampton. The first stopping place was at Madras, a city of four hundred thousand people, on the Bay of Bengal. This city was founded by the English, and hence there are but few Hindoo temples to be found here. But there are cathedrals, colleges, a museum, and an astronomical observatory. Our steamer was obliged to anchor two miles from the shore, as Madras has no harbor, and we could not get ashore, as the surf was so high that we did not deem the light, flat-bottomed boats (native name, *masulahs*) in which all must land, safe to intrust ourselves for such an adventure.

Madras, like Calcutta, has its native town of squalor and narrow streets, but the streets of the European part of the city are wide and handsome, and there are many elegant private residences on each side of these boulevards. This city carries on a large trade, but not so large as Calcutta. The favorite evening drive of the foreign residents of Madras is called Mount Road, and leads from the city to Mount St. Thome, where the apostle Thomas is said to have been buried. The Government House of Madras is a half oriental, half European palace, with spacious verandahs and Venetian blinds shutting out the heat of the sun.

Point de Galle, at the extreme southern point of Ceylon, was our next stopping place. Here we took a carriage and drove through the spice groves and inhaled the "spicy breezes which blow soft o'er Ceylon's isle." There is a high cone among the mountains of Ceylon called Adam's peak, which is visited by many pilgrims, who climb the steep sides by means of a chain fastened at the top. On the top of this steep rock there is something which looks like a footprint, and which the Buddhists say is a track of Buddha when he stepped from Ceylon to Siam. The Mohammedans think it is Adam's foot-mark when he was driven from the garden of Eden, hence the name Adam's peak. The uneducated Hindoos of Assam call the isle of Ceylon *Lonkadeep,* from the fact that they believe that *Lonka,* a great evil spirit, lives there, who devours every Hindoo who sets foot on its soil. The satin wood and the ebony are among the choice varieties of wood found in Ceylon. The most useful of all the trees is the cocoanut palm, which supplies the native with food, drink, house utensils, garden fences, torches and oil. The cinnamon groves are numerous, and the bark is a chief article of export. The cinnamon plant when growing wild is twenty or thirty feet high. Coffee is extensively cultivated. The inhabitants are Singalese, and the men have a curious custom of wearing round tortoise-shell combs to keep their long hair from falling over their faces. Point de Galle is quite a mart for turtles; we had some twenty of the monsters on board our steamer, and it was wonderful the enormous quantities of water they required to be thrown over them every day. Our captain said he was taking them to England to be made into soup. I did not measure them, but think they must have averaged three feet in width. All kinds of turtle-shell ware were brought on our steamer for sale, and eagerly bought by our passengers. Some of the combs and chains were very delicate and artistic in their mechanism.

We next touched at Aden, a strongly fortified

town belonging to Great Britain. It is in the southwest part of Arabia. Our ship dropped anchor at this port early in the morning, and the first sound we heard was the voice of a little boy in the adjoining cabin crying out to my little Henry: "Halloo, Henry, wake up! there are lots of little boys in the water with hair just like yours." We looked out of the window and saw a number of native boys, black shiny little fellows with hair bleached by water and sun until the color was nearer like taffy than anything else. Henry indignantly resented the assertion that his golden curls were to be likened to taffy, and very soiled taffy at that. The little taffy-headed boys come out in canoes and greet every steamer in order that they may dive for coin which the passengers throw to them in the water. They dive with wonderful agility, and often go underneath the large steamer and come up on the other side, displaying the new-found coin with exultant joy. It is an amusing sight, as these little glistening savages dive, to see for a while only the soles of their yellow feet, and after quite an interval their woolly pates emerging from the surface of the pale green water while the successful boy shows the shining coin between his teeth. For some reason, I know not what, the sharks never touch these little fellows.

Aden was produced by volcanic eruptions. Its highest peak is about one thousand feet. The harbor is good, and large depots of coal and other supplies are kept here for the British navy and passenger vessels. Rain falls but seldom, most of the water supply being condensed sea-water. There are tanks for receiving the water in case the rain falls. Aden is the gateway of the Red Sea, and our captain told us that the English were only one hour ahead of the French in taking possession of this, to them, important place. The heat was intense in the Red Sea, which we now entered, and as the full rays of the sun rested upon the water the play of colors was beautiful indeed. In the Gulf of Suez, the water is green, and the bay is edged with a border of bright yellow sand, and the top of the mountain ranges is red. Beautiful, indeed, and grand was the effect of these three colors so artistically arranged.

The Suez Canal, after ten years labor by thousands of workmen under the general superintendence of the distinguished engineer, M. Ferdinand de Lesseps, had but recently been opened, and our steamer made its way slowly, averaging about five miles an hour only. At Ismaila is a ferry across the canal to accommodate travellers from Jerusalem. This road may have been the path which Joseph and Mary and the infant Jesus took when fleeing into Egypt. Along the banks of the canal were many loaded camels driven by Arabs. I was much pleased with the little French cottages along the route of the canal, which were occupied by those caring for the canal. Though surrounded by the wide waste of sand these French people, always remarkable for their love of the beautiful, had flowers and vines growing about and over their cottages. It was a sight most restful to the eye wearied by the arid waste. While making our way through the canal we had a splendid opportunity of witnessing the wonderful deceptiveness of the mirage. Gazing out over the wide waste of burning sand, lovely lakes of water seemed spread out before us, and it was difficult to dispel the illusion. Even the most experienced camel-drivers are sometimes deceived by it, but our captain says the animals are never cheated in this way, as their sense of smell and other animal instincts always lead them aright. The Arabs call this illusion of the mirage the "sea that is not water." In India the mirage is sometimes called "the picture," and the "minstrel's white lake." There is an old Indian legend which tells of a minstrel who, being deceived by the appearance of sparkling fresh water, emptied out the contents of his water-bottle that he might fill it from the limpid stream. As a consequence he perished with thirst, and the moral is expressed in our English proverb: "A bird in the hand is worth two in the bush."

Port Said, with its long breakwater made of

artificial boulders of concrete, is next reached. Here the soil is all sand, and the coast low and monotonous in the extreme. A crowd of bare-legged turbaned natives and a few ugly dogs were all the signs of animate life to be seen, and we were glad to strike out to sea and breathe the invigorating air of the Mediterranean. Here we laid aside our thin clothes, and wrapped ourselves in flannels and blankets.

The city of Alexander the Great, bearing his illustrious name (Alexandria), next looms up before us. Cleopatra's needles then stood in bold relief, marking the place where the temple of Cæsar, the Cæsarim, stood. In 1877 one of these was presented by Mehemet Ali to the British, and was taken to London. The other Ismail Pasha gave to the United States of America, and in 1880 it was taken to New York. The red granite column known as Pompey's Pillar is Corinthian in its style of architecture, and is ninety-nine feet high, and makes a fine display as seen from the harbor. I have been told that a party of eight rollicking English sailors once flew a kite over the pillar and let it come down on the other side so that the string might fall from the top. They pulled up a rope with this string, and then the whole eight climbed to the top and drank punch and had a gay time, while the astonished Arabs gathered in a crowd to witness the strange and daring exploit.

We spent one day at rocky Malta, and went to the old church of the Knights of St. John. We were told an amusing story of a young man who was overquick in arriving at conclusions, who when he visited this church saw the women all dressed in black, and concluded that the men had all been killed in the Crimean war, and their widows, clad in the weeds of mourning, were at the church praying for the repose of their husbands' souls. He berated the English government roundly for thus drafting into military service so large a portion of the male population of Malta. He was quite taken aback when he was told that the costume of all the native women was the black one he had seen every woman in the church have on. This old church is grandly beautiful, with its special chapels for each country which sent out Crusaders. The floor is paved with marble slabs, on each of which is the name and title of a knight. The pictures on the walls are many of them the work of the French nuns, and are exquisitely embroidered on canvas. We were shown one that was said to be made from the broken threads which were cast aside from the embroidering of a larger picture. The work was very fine, and the general effect very pleasing, showing that even broken threads can be used by one who has a wise and good plan from which to work.

> "God takes our broken threads,
> And works them in
> With his own grand design;
> And in his sight
> All is complete
> Because begun with him."

Malta had an additional interest to us as being the island where the apostle Paul landed, and where the barbarous people showed him "no little kindness."

Great Britain's fortified rock, Gibraltar, engaged our next attention, but has been too often described by travellers to need any comment from me. This is said to be the only place in Europe were wild monkeys are found.

Six weeks from the day we left Calcutta we set foot on British ground at Southampton, and were soon seated in the coach for London. We had enjoyed a pleasant voyage; the cuisine, service and general attendance of our steamer were excellent. Ten days more passed and we were in our beloved native land, surrounded by friends from whom we had been long parted, and breathing in the June air made fragrant with roses.

CHAPTER XXII.

IMPRESSIONS OF AMERICA AFTER AN ABSENCE OF YEARS.

PAINFULLY impressed was I upon reaching America, with the nervous haste which seemed to characterize every man, woman and child. I felt inclined to stop every one whom I met and ask if a house was on fire, and, if not, why such desperate speed and restlessness? It tired me to see no calm people; nobody that had time for a social chat nor even time to eat their meals as they should be eaten.

Another thing that impressed me was the vast increase in the number of patent medicines, and I was forced to the conclusion that my native people were either a very "unhealthy people, or a very unhappy people, for their ills are either real or imaginary."

The immense foreign immigration which had gone on during my absence made me feel that our country was fast becoming the "pandemonium" of all nations. As I looked over the list of officers of our labor organizations I could find few English or American names, but Teutonic and Hibernian names everywhere abounded, and I was forced to ask the question: "Do our American people look upon manual labor as a disgrace?" When the great railroad strike came on, it seemed to me but a just punishment to our people for having given over their great labor organizations into foreign hands.

The increased number of suicides was a conviction forced upon me, in spite of all my determination to see only good in my dear native people. If the masses of our graduates from our public schools insist upon following after the professions, and a day dreaming idealism of wealth and high social position, how can we expect anything but hobbyists, cranks and insane hypochondriacs? Honest labor is the salvation of any race, and we can never expect to be a perfect people until we give up our wild pursuit of wealth gained by speculation and trickery, and learn to respect labor and the skilled artisan, and no longer give the highest social position to the millionaire, whether he has brains and morality or not.

I look upon the opening of numerous schools of technology all over our land at the present time as the dawning of an auspicious day, and hope that they may be crowded with pupils, while our law, medical and political aspirants may be reduced to the few who are adapted to their professions, and who will do their work faithfully and well. The disposition of the young people to take their marriage affairs into their own hands, and the consequent increase of divorce cases in our courts, was another thing that impressed me unfavorably on my return to my country.

But there were also bright and cheering impressions; the broad and liberal attitude of our churches in the way of frowning down human creeds and denominational bigotry, and the showing of true love and sympathy for all who bore the image of Christ, was one of the most inspiring of all these favorable impressions. My countrymen had come nearer realizing the true idea of the Fatherhood of God and the Brotherhood of man.

This spirit showed itself in philanthropies broad and far reaching, extending even to the uttermost parts of the earth. "The kindly feeling, the desire to help, the increased skill which springs up under Christianity, as flowers and fruits grow in the sunshine," were to me at once a refreshing and a solace. These things "are not miracles, but are better than miracles, as the prolonged sunshine is better than the flash of lightning." I found the day laborer of my native land enjoying more books, libraries, railroads, telegraphs and newspapers, than the Rajahs and Ranis of India. At the present time the philanthropies of our United States amount to $120,000,000 annually, and care for orphans, waifs, insane, sick, little wanderers, cripples, drunken outcasts, and children, and those needing reformations; while we have forty-three institutions for the deaf and dumb which average 5,743 inmates annually; thirty blind asylums, with 2,178 annually taught and cared for; and eleven institutions which care for idiots, with 1,781 yearly inmates. In New York city alone the charitable societies expend each year $4,000,000. Surely this is a showing of liberality such as no un-Christian country could ever exhibit. Add to these all that is being done in heathen lands through the instrumentality of American money and American workers, and we have reason to be proud of the record, and should strive still to further increase our philanthropic and Christian efforts. God forbid that our beloved land should ever prove recreant to her high trust, and place herself on the side of agnosticism and atheism, for:

"Once to every man and nation comes the moment to decide
In the strife of truth with falsehood, for the good or evil side;
Some great cause, God's new Messiah, offering each the bloom or blight,
Parts the goats upon the left hand, and the sheep upon the right,
And the chance goes by forever, 'twixt the darkness and the light."

My children enjoyed the new and beautiful life that came to them with the June roses, under a sun that did not light upon them with a tropical heat, and the lovely Autumn tints, and with the frost and snow.

Our national holidays were times of great interest to them, as they had known nothing of fire-crackers, Roman candles and sky-rockets in Assam. Their efforts at the English language were amusing, for, in spite of all my efforts, I had never been able to get them to speak English in Assam, and even when I would tell them a story in that language they would beg of me to talk to them in their own Assamese tongue. The termination for the future tenses in the Assamese language is *ibo*, and when they wished to say "it will rain, snow or hail," they would put it in the form of "rainibo," "snowibo" and "hailibo." And even after they learned the English words they would cling to the Assamese idioms and order of expression. Instead of saying, "Please, give me a drink of water," they would form the sentence thus: "To me, water give, please." And instead of saying, "I don't like the cold weather," they would say, "I like cold weather, no, not so." The first anniversary of George Washington's birthday after our return excited little Henry's curious interest, and he asked me why it was that they did not have school that day. I told him because it was George Washington's birthday. He inquired in return if "George would have his washing done every day," adding that he hoped he would, as he liked to play better than to go to school. When I explained to him all about the illustrious "father of his country," and told him that he had long been dead, but that a grateful people loved to honor his memory, the little fellow only remarked, that George must have had a great deal of soiled linen if it had not all been washed yet. He could not get the name Washington into his little head, for he had never been used to hearing two names given to one person.

The sensation of cold from handling ice and snow my children invariably called heat, and said they were "burnt with the ice." Before the end of the first winter at home, however, they had adjusted themselves to their new surroundings, and had acquired the language so as to speak it without a brogue.

As I review the years of my residence abroad, I am persuaded that they have been the golden days of my life as far as true usefulness is concerned; and if you ask me to tell you in detail why the work of a missionary in India is grand and noble, let me answer you in the language of the British House of Commons:

"Apart from their special duties as public preachers and pastors, the foreign missionaries constitute a valuable body of educators; they contribute greatly to the cultivation of the native languages and literature; all who are resident in rural districts are appealed to for help of a medical character. They have prepared hundreds of works suited both for schools and for general circulation in the fifteen most prominent languages of India, and in several other districts they are the compilers of several dictionaries and grammars. They have written important works on the native classics and the system of philosophy; and they have largely stimulated the great increase of native literature prepared in recent years by educated native gentlemen. A great increase has taken place in the number of converts the last twenty years. They number now at least five hundred thousand. The government of India cannot but acknowledge the great obligation under which it is laid by these benevolent exertions of these six hundred missionaries, whose blameless lives and self-denying labors are infusing new vigor into the stereotyped life of the great populations placed under English rule, and are preparing them to be in every way better men and better citizens of the great empire in which they dwell." And to this let me add the testimony of one who is well prepared to speak on this subject: "The wide diffusion of Christian knowledge; the arousing of the Hindoo mind from its long torpor to the earnest discussion of the merits and claims of Christianity; the abolition of Suttee, of female infanticide, and hook-swinging; the loosing of the bonds of caste, the diminished influence of Brahminical powers, and the earnest desire and practical efforts put forth for the education of women, all show that India's long night of superstition and moral ignorance is passing away, and the dawn of a glorious day already at hand."

It is an honor to any human being to have had a hand and heart in this great work of saving a nation.

CHAPTER XXIII.

WHY RETURN TO ASSAM?

WHEN I left my home in the beautiful green valley of the Brahmapootra river, I little thought that more than a decade and a half of years would pass away before I should return thither.

But finding that my children required my presence and care, and fully realizing that no higher and nobler life could possibly engage my heart than a mother's mission for her children bereft of a father, I have stayed on, year after year, and have been very happy in my work and my surroundings. The time has come when my fostering care is no longer needed for my children, since they have come to fill their own places in the busy world, among the bread-winners, where they are serving Christ and his cause; and they cheerfully consent for me to go back to my unfinished work in India.

When one has for years pursued a certain line of work, amid surroundings pleasant and satisfactory, in their own beloved land, the question very naturally suggests itself, "Why make a change? Why go to a foreign land and to a heathen people? Are the reasons which lead to this change sufficiently weighty to warrant such a step?" Many times have these questions been put to me since I decided to return, and I deem it but due to the dear friends of my native land to answer them honestly and frankly in this closing chapter of my book.

First. My presence is desired there; I have the confidence and affection of the natives; and their language is almost as familiar to me as my own mother tongue.

When I was left alone in the mission after my husband's death, a company of native women, fearing I would be lonely, came night after night, bringing with them their babies, and stayed with me. It was their way of showing their affection and sympathy, and I most thoroughly appreciated their motives. Nor could I feel alone with a dozen babies in the house besides my own little children. Many incidents such as the following also go to prove that these poor Assamese women loved me and wished me to live among them. A hill tribe woman whose son had been in our Normal School, and who had heard Mr. Marston preach Christ's words on the mountains, on hearing of the death of the preacher, came eleven days' journey through dense jungles infested with wild and savage animals, that she might mingle her tears with mine. On reaching my bungalow she said, with tears streaming down her cheeks, "I know what it is to lose one's right arm. I, too, am a widow, and I have come from my mountain home to tell you how deeply I sympathize with you."

When I bade adieu to the company of native pupils, Bible women, school-teachers, native preachers, and Hindoo and hill people who had been about me during the twelve years of my sojourn in Assam, they were sorely grieved at the parting, and Korno Siga was spokesman for the whole company in words which I have given you in a previous chapter. Sixteen years have passed, and month by month he and his waiting company ask almost piteously: "Are you not coming back very soon?"

Second. I am needed in Assam a hundredfold more than here in my own land. Teachers and physicians crowd against each other here on every hand. There I shall have the consciousness that I am doing a work which would otherwise be left undone, for the harvest is great and the laborers are few and scattered. I could tell heart-rending stories of the sad condition of our dark Hindoo sisters who are compelled to live on in sickness and suffering because the custom of the country forbids them to be seen by gentlemen physicians. The Christian lady physician has, therefore, a wider field of usefulness in India than in America. When I left Assam there was not, in all that province, a Zenana in which I was not cordially welcomed, and I was free to talk to those poor, ignorant, though beautiful women, of the grand truths of a saving Christianity. By kind and patient attention to their physical needs, by attending them in their hours of sickness and pain, and by an expressed practical interest in their homes and home life, one may so gain their confidence that they will listen to the more important things which pertain to their souls' eternal welfare. Lady Dufferin is doing a most noble work in India in establishing lady physicians who shall take charge of hospitals for women and children, and train a corps of native nurses to care for the sick of their own sex.

Our lady missionary physicians are doing a still more important work, caring for both soul and body. And our Indian sisters begin to appreciate the value of this work which meets a long-felt need. I candidly believe that I am needed there for just such work as this.

Third. I return to Assam because I believe it to be the duty and privilege of individuals, as well as of nations, to work out their highest destiny. Service for the divine Christ is, I believe, the highest destiny of mortals, as well as of angels. "Life is the exertion of power," and spiritual life, which is the highest form of life, is the exertion of spiritual power to benefit humanity. This spiritual power is generated in the heart of every one who drinks of the fountain of eternal life, and is made a new creature in Christ. Feeling assured that my life will be of more service to the Saviour's cause in Assam than it can be here, and believing that the line of my highest destiny lies in this direction, I again turn my face to the Orient.

Fourth, and most important of all my reasons. I return to Assam because I believe that Christianity is the vital power for the salvation of her sons and daughters. Assured that Christ's religion has in it an infinitely higher morality and spirituality, and consequently an infinitely greater power to save humanity than Buddhism, Brahminism, or any New Brotherhood of Robert Elsmere, I count it a joy and a privilege to bear the news of a crucified and risen Jesus to those who grope in thick darkness.

Not that I think that God has left himself without witnesses during all these years in India. I cannot believe that. But as Buddhism, the so-called "Light of Asia," is agnosticism and atheism, surely this religion has not been God's best manifestation. And as Brahminism is gross idolatry and licentiousness, we can hardly call *this*, God's chosen means of manifesting himself to India. The apostle Paul tells us plainly in the first chapter of Romans, that God's eternal power and Godhead have been clearly shown to them, so that they are without excuse. And we are told also in the first chapter of John's Gospel that the true light lighteth every man that cometh into the world. But it is a sad fact, made very manifest to those who have lived among heathen peoples, that the truth of God has been changed by them into falsehood, and their hearts have been darkened by sin until the "unknown God" needs to be declared to them with the earnest power which Christ's life and atonement can alone make effectual to their salvation.

The missionary work is not simply a philanthropy, nor is it simply an inspiration caught from the life of a pure noble man who lived eighteen hundred years ago, and suffered martyrdom for his principles by death on the Roman cross. If I believed that Christ was only a good man, I should not consider it my duty to leave my children and my beloved native land to go to Assam. Sacredly and reverently I believe that "God commended his love toward us in that while we were yet sinners Christ died for us," and that "whosoever believeth on him shall not perish but have everlasting life."

This Jesus who is the "Light of the World," in whom is the hope of all nations, has said, "go teach all nations," and it is for us to obey the heavenly vision.

We would esteem no man a true patriot who would refuse to represent his country in a foreign court; we would consider no man a true lover of his country who would refuse to fight his country's battles when her voice called loudly for his help. Even so, should the soldiers of Christ hold themselves ready for any service their commander may demand of them, whether that service be at home or in a foreign country. The true missionary spirit is one of lowliness and ready service.

By obedience to the divine will, by an earnest sympathy with the common people, by going on his missions, by giving freely our property and ourselves to advance his cause, thus can we show forth the true missionary spirit, in whatever land we are called to do our life-work.

And *lastly*. I return to Assam because I earnestly desire to add my mite toward carrying on the work so nobly begun by our martyr heroes who have fallen in the battle. From the days of the sainted Thomas, who died when but within sight of his mission field in Assam, down to the present time, there have been noble men and women who have joyfully given their full ten talents, their time, and their most faithful service to this work, and have laid down their lives for it. They have accomplished a great work, but that mission is now in a very needy condition and calls loudly for reinforcement. I cannot call the work of these Assamese martyrs an unfinished work, for is not "man immortal until his work is done?" But we have an unfinished work there, and a divine obligation rests upon us to do what we can do towards its completion.

Scattered laborers strong in faith are toiling on amid the whitened fields of Assam, while ever and anon one falls by the way, and there seem no workers ready to seize the fallen sickle and gather the grain. Pray ye the Lord of the harvest to send forth more laborers into this most needy field.

> "Hark, the voice of Jesus calling,
> Who will go and work to-day?
> Fields are white, the harvest waiting,
> Who will bear the sheaves away?
> Loud and long the Master calleth,
> Rich reward he offers you:
> Who will answer, gladly saying,
> Here am I, O Lord, send me."

"Why return to Assam?"

First. My presence is desired there.

Second. I am needed there.

Third. Service for Christ in that land lies in the line of my highest destiny.

Fourth. Christianity is the vital and saving power of all nations, and Christ bids us, "Go teach all nations."

Fifth. The noble army of martyrs who have begun a great work in Assam call upon us to carry that work to a glorious completion.

To the beloved friends who have made my stay in America so delightsome, I commend my children and my lovely little grand-daughter, while I turn my face to the land of the Rising Sun, to my husband's grave, to my unfinished work, and to that faithful company, who, with Korno Siga, wait and watch for me on the brow of the hill.

From thence I may send back some notes of "Assam revisited."

14

THE END.